G000244119

LEICESTER CITY FC

MISCELLANY

LEICESTER CITY FC
MISCELLANY

DAVID CLAYTON

AMBERLEY

For Samantha, Pablo and little Valentina, with much love x

First published 2014

Amberley Publishing
The Hill, Stroud, Gloucestershire, GL5 4EP
www.amberley-books.com

Copyright © David Clayton, 2014

The right of David Clayton to be identified as the Author
of this work has been asserted in accordance with the
Copyrights, Designs and Patents Act 1988.

All rights reserved. No part of this book may be reprinted
or reproduced or utilised in any form or by any electronic,
mechanical or other means, now known or hereafter invented,
including photocopying and recording, or in any information
storage or retrieval system, without the permission in writing
from the Publishers.

British Library Cataloguing in Publication Data.
A catalogue record for this book is available from the British Library.

ISBN 978 1 4456 4222 2 (print)
ISBN 978 1 4456 4244 4 (ebook)

Typesetting by Amberley Publishing.
Printed in Great Britain.

CONTENTS

ACKNOWLEDGEMENTS

Thanks to the countless journalists, programme editors and supporters who committed their thoughts to print over the years, and everyone who has unknowingly played a part in the creation of this book – too many to thank personally, but I thank you all nonetheless.

One thing I didn't do was consult Matt Bozeat's *Leicester City Miscellany* when I was asked to write this book. I decided that, though it would be the ideal place to find added inspiration when I needed it, it would have been too tempting to delve into it often and be lazy on my part. Hopefully, if you have both miscellany books, that will be clear enough, though I can't believe we won't have covered a number of similar findings. If there's any justice, both mine and Dave's will be must-have purchases for any respectable City fan.

My cross-reference rock throughout was *Of Fossils & Foxes* by Dave Smith and Paul Taylor – probably the best fact-based history book I've ever come across. Fantastic work gents, and invaluable to have such a tome on hand when coming across any sketchy details.

Thanks to several websites, too, including 11v11, Leicester City Footy Mad, Statto.com, LTID, Historical Kits, and snippets and quotes from interviews by writers like Henry Winter. Thanks to all the people associated with those websites and newspapers. I hope I've not forgotten anyone and I made attempts to contact anyone I've used snippets from. Again, many thanks to all the unaccredited writers that gave me inspiration during a very hectic writing schedule.

I've written a number of books on football clubs, but I really enjoyed researching the Foxes' history and finding out so much about a team that has contributed so much to English football and produced so many household names over the years. Promotion back to the Premier League has given City a real chance to not only rub shoulders with the great and good, but perhaps take a place among them on a more permanent basis – something that hasn't been the case for far too long. It's about time there was fresh blood at the top table and, with such proud traditions, the Foxes have earned the right to pitch for a place of their own.

Finally, thanks to Tom Furby at Amberley Publishing for giving me the opportunity to write about Leicester City Football Club, and also to my wife and three kids who I had to sacrifice precious time with as the deadline loomed. I hope you, the reader, enjoys the book and, even if it's saved for those precious quiet few minutes in the smallest room in the house, that's good enough for me.

David Clayton
July 2014

LEICESTER CITY FC MISCELLANY

SUNDAY BEST

On 4 December 1983, the Foxes played their first match on a Sunday with a trip to Brian Clough's Nottingham Forest. Goals from Robert Jones and Alan Smith were not enough to prevent a defeat at the City Ground, Gordon Milne's men going down 3-2.

TOP TEN APPEARANCES FOR CITY

Here are the men who served the Foxes with great pride over many years – the record appearance holders:

Graham Cross	599
Sep Smith	586
Adam Black	557
Hugh Adcock	460
Mark Wallington	460
Willie Frame	459
Steve Walsh	448
Mal Griffiths	420
Arthur Chandler	419
John Sjoberg	413

ABANDONED SHIP

A total of eighteen games involving the Foxes have been called off for one reason or another. Seven times the reason was a waterlogged pitch, while fog is the next largest culprit, accounting for five abandonments. Snow took two matches, while ice or frost was the reason another match didn't reach a conclusion. Other reasons have been gale force winds, floodlight failure and in 2007, Clive Clarke suffered heart failure during a League Cup second round tie away to Nottingham Forest. City were winning six of the games, drawing in seven of them and losing another five. Since 1974, in the six matches cancelled, the Foxes had failed to score.

The full list is:

1894	Division Two	v. Darwen (a)	0-0	2 mins	Gale-force winds
1895	Division Two	v. Newton H (a)	0-2	65 mins	Waterlogged
1901	Division Two	v. Blackpool (h)	1-0	67 mins	Fog
1903	Division Two	v. Man United (a)	2-1	78 mins	Fog
1905	Division Two	v. Burnley (a)	0-1	79 mins	Waterlogged
1914	FA Cup	v. Norwich (h)	0-0	65 mins	Snow
1931	Division One	v. Portsmouth (h)	1-0	63 mins	Fog
1933	Division One	v. Birmingham (a)	2-1	66 mins	Fog
1934	Division One	v. Chelsea (a)	1-1	78 mins	Fog
1936	Division Two	v. Newcastle U (h)	2-1	80 mins	Snow
1961	FA Cup	v. Bristol City (h)	0-0	45 mins	Waterlogged
1967	Division One	v. Notts Forest (a)	1-0	51 mins	Frost
1974	Division One	v. 'Boro (h)	0-1	24 mins	Floodlight failure
1983	Division One	v. Southampton (h)	0-0	22 mins	Waterlogged
2003	Division One	v. Reading (a)	0-0	45 mins	Waterlogged
2005	Championship	v. Burnley (a)	0-0	19 mins	Waterlogged
2005	Championship	v. Plymouth (a)	0-1	45 mins	Waterlogged
2007	League Cup	v. Notts Forest (a)	0-1	45 mins	Medical reasons

CLIVE CLARKE: QUOTE/UNQUOTE

City's on-loan striker, Clive Clarke, after recovering from a cardiac arrest during the half-time break against Nottingham Forest in August 2007:

> I remember feeling a bit lethargic on the field in the first half, and I was involved in a collision with our goalkeeper Paul Henderson, which led to their goal. I sat quietly in a corner of the dressing room and felt a bit queasy. I can recall Patrick Kisnorbo talking to me, but it wasn't really registering. Then I just passed out. When I was told what had happened, the blood drained from my body. I just thought I could have been dead, and that I might never have seen my family again. When you think about Sevilla player Antonio Puerta (who collapsed last Saturday and died on Tuesday), it goes without saying that a day won't pass when I don't cherish every moment in my life.

Ian Holloway reflects on a turbulent, yet educational time as City boss, September 2012:

> My time at Leicester helped me with my life and really helped me with my next job at Blackpool. I wouldn't be doing what I'm doing here without what happened to me at Leicester. I can guarantee Leicester fans that every single day I went into that club I tried my best. Whatever I seemed to do there didn't really work, but there wasn't one day I gave up – not ever. It was like my worst nightmare ever. Leicester are a great club, the fans didn't moan at me much when I was there. I've learnt from that awful feeling and I was strong enough to look at what I did, dust myself down and get back going.

Milan Mandaric responds to criticism from Colin Hall, the Mayor of Leicester, after he claimed a 6-1 defeat to Portsmouth 'shamed the city' in October 2010:

The Lord Mayor was a candidate for the manager's position because he knows so much about football and managing the club! I was disappointed not to give him that chance. He is a nice man but he probably doesn't know how much I have done for the club, my commitments and how much I have sacrificed for this club.

Kasabian's Serge Pizzorno taking a bit of reverse psychology on board back in 2005:

The great thing about Leicester City is we're s**t. We are absolutely rubbish. But that doesn't matter because every so often when we do achieve something; it's all the sweeter after so much suffering. It must be an absolute nightmare being a Manchester United fan these days because you're following a team that's just become a profit-making company. Imagine if you're a fan from Stretford and you've supported them for twenty years, from before they were good. You can't just turn your back on them because they're your team, so it must break your heart to see what they've become. It's the same with Chelsea. I'd hate it if that ever happened to City, if we ever became about making money. I'd rather support a s**t team. I'm proud to be s**t.

FOX ON THE BOX

In today's saturated television coverage of football, it's hard to imagine what it must have been like when no games at all were televised and the radio and newspaper reports were all fans had to go on, as well as the odd appearance on Pathe News. Of course, as time went on, selected games began to appear on various programmes and it was inevitable the Foxes would eventually appear on the box. On 12 November 1955, BBC's *Sportsweek* showed highlights of the game between Leicester *v.* Swansea Town – it proved a good omen, too, with the Foxes winning 6-1. Nine years later, City's debut on *Match of the Day* came with a 3-2 win over Nottingham Forest on 17 October 1964. Sky were the first to broadcast City playing live during a Full Member's Cup tie against Wolves at Filbert Street in November 1990. The visitors won 1-0.

MILLION-POUND MAN

Midfielder Mark Draper was City's first £1 million signing when he moved to Filbert Street in July 1994. Draper made his name with Notts County, for whom he played more than 200 games between 1988 and 1994 and cost an initial £1.25 million, which would rise a further £500,000 if certain criteria were met. He missed a penalty against Newcastle United on his full debut and made forty-three appearances for the Foxes during the 1994/95 season, but couldn't prevent relegation after just one season back in the top flight. He scored five goals – all in the Premier League – but when Aston Villa made a bid of £3.25 million, City decided to cash in to the tine of a £2 million profit.

THE GREATEST

To celebrate 125 years of the Football League during the 2013/14 season, FL125.co.uk ran a series of 'best-ever' votes via twitter to find out the Foxes' champions. They wrote:

The FL125 Greatest Captain voting shortlists were compiled from data submitted by Football League clubs, which was collected from fans through social media. Supporters were asked to submit their suggestions by interacting with their respective clubs through Twitter, using #FL125 and #OurBestCaptain. Here are the results of each vote:

Q: Who is Leicester City's best ever captain?

The nominees were:

Steve Walsh: Captained City for much of the 1990s. Captain for much of Brian Little's time (but not 1994 play-off final), for Martin O'Neill's 1996 play-off final winners, and for 1997 and 1999 League Cup finals, winning in 1997.

Matt Elliott: Captained Leicester to League Cup win at Wembley in 2000.

David Nish: Captained Leicester to FA Cup final (youngest-ever captain in FA Cup final history) in 1969 and to Second Division title (1971).

Colin Appleton: Captained the Foxes in 1963 FA Cup final, the 1964 League Cup final (winners) and 1965 League Cup final. Also captained Leicester to their second highest ever league position (fourth in 1963).

Johnny Duncan: Captained Leicester to Second Division title (1925) and then to within one point of winning the old First Division title (1929).

Result:

Rank	Player	Percentage
1	Steve Walsh	59%
2	Matt Elliott	26%
3	David Nish	6%
3	Colin Appleton	6%
4	Johnny Duncan	3%

Q: Who is Leicester City's greatest-ever player?

The nominees were:

Gordon Banks: Arguably the greatest goalkeeper to ever play the game, Banks played for Leicester City for eight years, winning the World Cup with England during that time. Played in two League Cup finals and two FA Cup finals for the Foxes.

Arthur Chandler: The club's record goalscorer, he scored 273 goals in 419 games between 1923 and 1935, including seventeen hat-tricks – another club record.

Keith Weller: One of the most popular, talented and entertaining players in the club's history, Weller lit up the Jimmy Bloomfield era between 1971 and 1978. Scorer and creator of some of the Foxes' most iconic goals.

Sep Smith: The club's longest-serving player, Sep spent twenty seasons with the Foxes and made 373 first class appearances between 1929 and 1949. But for the Second World War, he surely would have passed the club's all-time appearance record. A City legend, regarded among those who saw him as among the greatest to wear the shirt.

Steve Walsh: The embodiment of the passion and commitment demanded by the City faithful in the 1980s and '90s. Walsh played in six out of seven Wembley appearances the club made from 1992–2000, winning promotion to the Premier League in 1994 and 1996, and lifting the League Cup as captain in 1997.

Rank	Player	Percentage
1	Gordon Banks	37%
2	Steve Walsh	32%
3	Keith Weller	20%
4	Arthur Chandler	8%
5	Sep Smith	3%

Q: Who was the Foxes' Leicester City's best-ever manager?

The nominees:

Peter Hodge: Laid the foundations for the club's first golden age in the 1920s.

Matt Gillies: He was City's manager for ten years in the top flight (1958-68). Led the Foxes to FA Cup finals in 1961 and 1963. Guided them to League Cup success in 1964, and finished as runners-up in the same competition a year later.

Johnny Duncan: A former club captain who went on to lead the club into its first FA Cup final as manager in 1949.

Brian Little: Took over with club rock bottom of Division Two in 1991. Reached three successive play-off finals, culminating in promotion to the Premier League in 1994.

Martin O'Neill: Won promotion to the Premier League in 1996 and went on to achieve four successive top-ten finishes in the top flight. Leicester were League Cup winners in 1997 and 2000 under O'Neill, as well as League Cup finalists in 1999.

Result:

Rank	Manager	Percentage
1	Martin O'Neill	86%
2	Matt Gillies	7%
3	Brian Little	4%
4	Peter Hodge	2%
5	Johnny Duncan	1%

NOT CHANDLER AGAIN...?

The mere sight of prolific City goalscorer Arthur Chandler was enough to send shivers down the spine of any Aston Villa fan. Chandler is the only player in Foxes history to have scored a hat-trick of hat-tricks against one club – namely Aston Villa. Chandler, who scored an incredible 273 goals in 419 appearances, bagged five against Villa in one game as he continued his one-man demolition job against the Birmingham side during his twelve-year stay with the Foxes.

MAKE MINE A TREBLE

Fred Shinto holds a record that is unlikely to be beaten anytime soon. In November 1909, Shinton nagged a five-minute hat-trick – the quickest treble in City history. The Foxes won the game 3-0, and it's a pity only 1,000 people were at Filbert Street to see the feat. Those who were there witnessed a record that has lasted 105 years – and counting! Then known as Fosse, Shinton's stay with the club was fairly brief, but in 101 appearances he racked up a very impressive fifty-eight goals – one of the Foxes best-ever goals-per-game ratios.

MARTIN O'NEILL: QUOTE/UNQUOTE

Some words of wit and wisdom from our most successful boss to date.

After a poor start, O'Neill warns the board not to expect miracles:

> But if there was any talking to be done, I wanted to have my say. And I had my say and, I hope, they listened. It was a frank discussion. I said I'd only been there for three months. That I needed some time and that things were not quite as rosy as they might have seemed here.

O'Neill pledges promotion, but reins in expectations:

> I said it might not happen this season, but it would happen – Leicester City would be in the Premiership. And then we went on a little run.

LCFC and Martin O'Neill, a match made in heaven:

> I loved it there. I put my heart and soul into the club. It was as if Leicester City Football club was my club, my baby.

Teething problems for O'Neill at Filbert Street:

Quite a few of the players were not happy. They seemed to think that Mark McGhee would be back for them and they would follow him to Wolves. There was a lot of disillusionment because many of the players got on so well with McGhee. They didn't want to be at the club. And some of them did go. Steve Corica, for instance – I think there was a myth growing up around him. He had some good games at the start of the season but I think he thought he was a better player than he was. He caused a bit of hassle and left quite quickly. He went to Wolves. I allowed him to go – but by then I had Lennon and I was looking to get Izzet.

Martin O'Neill – gone from LCFC but not forgotten:

As J. F. Kennedy once said, the torch passes on. It's up to someone else. But I loved it there. I had five of the best years of my life there.

SHIRT SPONSORS AND KIT MAKERS

The first shirt sponsorship deal for City was in 1983, when Ind Coope became the shirt sponsors after penning a three-year deal. Bukta were the first kit manufacturers while the longest shirt sponsor to date has been Walkers, who were the name on the players' shirts from 1987 to 2001.

Period	Kit Sponsor	Shirt Sponsor
1962–1964	Bukta	
1976–1979	Admiral	
1979–1983	Umbro	
1983–1986	Admiral	Ind Coope
1986/1987	John Bull	
1987/1988	Walkers	
1988–1990	Scoreline	

1990–1992	Bukta	
1992–2000	Fox Leisure	
2000/2001	Le Coq Sportif	
2001–2003	LG	
2003–2005	Alliance & Leicester	
2005–2007	JJB	
2007–2009	Jako	Topps Tiles
2009/2010	Joma	Jessops (rear of home shirt)
		Loros (away shirt only)
2010–2012	Burrda	King Power
2012–Present	Puma	

AFRICAN KING

Arthur Chandler took part in three Test matches for an FA XI against South Africa in 1929 and was the star man in each match. Played during the close season before the 1929/30 campaign, the FA XI secured an opening victory in Durban, beating the Springboks 3-2 – Chandler was on the mark twice. Almost a month later, Chandler scored another brace as the FA XI beat South Africa 2-1 in Johannesburg. Four days later, it was the City man again at the double as the FA XI secured a 3-1 whitewash. Six goals in three games – Chandler was a scoring machine at any level.

JEEPERS 'KEEPERS

City have been blessed with some truly world class goalkeepers over the years and arguably two of England's best ever in Gordon Banks and Peter Shilton. But of all our shot-stoppers, who has the best ratio of keeping the opposition out? Here are the top ten:

Player	Apps	Goals	Average goals conceded per game
Peter Shilton	339	379	1.118
George Hebden	104	118	1.135
Kasper Schmeichel	156	178	1.141
Kasey Keller	125	143	1.144
Ian Walker	156	205	1.314
Mark Wallington	460	607	1.319
Herbert Brown	154	211	1.370
Kevin Poole	193	278	1.440
Jimmy Thraves	148	215	1.453
Gordon Banks	356	529	1.486
Ian Andrews	139	238	1.712
Sandy McLaren	256	448	1.750
Johnny Anderson	277	488	1.762

THE M69 DERBY

With only 24 miles separating the cities of Leicester and Coventry, the Sky Blues are always going to be one of the Foxes' main rivals, even if the game doesn't have the same vitriol and adrenaline rush of City *v.* Forest. The teams first met in 1919 and have clashed a total of eighty-two times to date ,with City winning thirty-seven and Coventry twenty-five. Here is our complete record against the Sky Blues:

Championship

3 March 2012	Leicester City 2-0 Coventry City
6 August 2011	Coventry City 0-1 Leicester City
26 February 2011	Leicester City 1-1 Coventry City
11 September 2010	Coventry City 1-1 Leicester City
21 March 2010	Leicester City 2-2 Coventry City
3 October 2009	Coventry City 1-1 Leicester City

23 February 2008	Coventry City 2-0 Leicester City
12 January 2008	Leicester City 2-0 Coventry City
17 February 2007	Leicester City 3-0 Coventry City
18 August 2006	Coventry City 0-0 Leicester City
17 April 2006	Coventry City 1-1 Leicester City
23 October 2005	Leicester City 2-1 Coventry City
8 November 2004	Leicester City 3-0 Coventry City
16 October 2004	Coventry City 1-1 Leicester City

English Division One

| 22 March 2003 | Coventry City 1-2 Leicester City |
| 29 October 2002 | Leicester City 2-1 Coventry City |

Premier League

7 April 2001	Leicester City 1-3 Coventry City
10 December 2000	Coventry City 1-0 Leicester City
27 November 1999	Coventry City 0-1 Leicester City
11 October 1999	Leicester City 1-0 Coventry City
24 April 1999	Leicester City 1-0 Coventry City
28 November 1998	Coventry City 1-1 Leicester City
4 April 1998	Leicester City 1-1 Coventry City
29 November 1997	Coventry City 0-2 Leicester City
8 March 1997	Coventry City 0-0 Leicester City
21 December 1996	Leicester City 0-2 Coventry City
25 February 1995	Coventry City 4-2 Leicester City
3 October 1994	Leicester City 2-2 Coventry City

Division One (old)

4 May 1987	Leicester City 1-1 Coventry City
6 December 1986	Coventry City 1-0 Leicester City
8 March 1986	Leicester City 2-1 Coventry City
6 October 1985	Coventry City 3-0 Leicester City
23 December 1984	Leicester City 5-1 Coventry City
1 September 1984	Coventry City 2-0 Leicester City

21 January 1984	Leicester City 1-1 Coventry City
17 September 1983	Coventry City 2-1 Leicester City
14 March 1981	Coventry City 4-1 Leicester City
11 October 1980	Leicester City 1-3 Coventry City
11 March 1978	Coventry City 1-0 Leicester City
15 October 1977	Leicester City 1-2 Coventry City
12 March 1977	Leicester City 3-1 Coventry City
2 October 1976	Coventry City 1-1 Leicester City
3 April 1976	Coventry City 0-2 Leicester City
27 September 1975	Leicester City 0-3 Coventry City
15 March 1975	Coventry City 2-2 Leicester City
28 September 1974	Leicester City 0-1 Coventry City
22 December 1973	Coventry City 1-2 Leicester City
29 September 1973	Leicester City 0-2 Coventry City
6 January 1973	Coventry City 3-2 Leicester City
26 October 1972	Leicester City 0-0 Coventry City
22 April 1972	Leicester City 1-0 Coventry City
4 December 1971	Coventry City 1-1 Leicester City
1 April 1969	Coventry City 1-0 Leicester City
28 September 1968	Leicester City 1-1 Coventry City
27 April 1968	Coventry City 0-1 Leicester City
2 December 1967	Leicester City 0-0 Coventry City

Division Two (old)

8 March 1952	Coventry City 1-3 Leicester City
20 October 1951	Leicester City 3-1 Coventry City
3 February 1951	Leicester City 3-0 Coventry City
23 September 1950	Coventry City 2-1 Leicester City
27 December 1949	Coventry City 1-2 Leicester City
26 December 1949	Leicester City 1-0 Coventry City
1 January 1949	Leicester City 3-1 Coventry City
28 October 1948	Coventry City 1-2 Leicester City
17 January 1948	Leicester City 2-2 Coventry City
6 September 1947	Coventry City 0-1 Leicester City

10 May 1947	Coventry City 2-1 Leicester City
19 October 1946	Leicester City 1-0 Coventry City
25 February 1937	Coventry City 0-2 Leicester City
17 October 1936	Leicester City 1-0 Coventry City
24 January 1925	Leicester City 5-1 Coventry City
20 September 1924	Coventry City 4-2 Leicester City
23 February 1924	Leicester City 2-0 Coventry City
16 February 1924	Coventry City 2-4 Leicester City
24 March 1923	Coventry City 1-1 Leicester City
17 March 1923	Leicester City 2-1 Coventry City
26 November 1921	Leicester City 1-1 Coventry City
19 November 1921	Coventry City 0-0 Leicester City
29 March 1921	Coventry City 1-0 Leicester City
28 March 1921	Leicester City 0-1 Coventry City
4 October 1919	Coventry City 1-2 Leicester City
27 September 1919	Leicester City 1-0 Coventry City

FA Cup

23 January 1999 (round four)	Leicester City 0-3 Coventry City
14 January 1952 (round three replay)	Coventry City 4-1 Leicester City
12 January 1952 (round three)	Leicester City 1-1 Coventry City

League Cup

1 December 1964 (round five)	Coventry City 1-8 Leicester City

Complete Record

Leicester City: Played 82, Won 37, Drawn 24, Lost 25, For 121, Against 98

CITY'S SHORTEST SEASON

The Foxes' shortest-ever season was in 1939/40, when, following a 4-3 win over Manchester City, a 2-0 defeat away to Birmingham City and a 2-0 home win over West Ham United, the Football League programme was suspended due to the outbreak of the Second World War. City were in fifth position in Division Two at the time. When the war ended, the matches were replayed and City again conceded three goals at home to Manchester City, though this time without reply in a demoralising 0-3 defeat. Birmingham doubled the margin of their previous victory with a 4-0 win at St Andrew's with only the 2-0 win over West Ham replicated.

DOUBLE TROUBLE

'Make mine a double' may be a popular phrase in the bar, but for a goalkeeper, it is the stuff of nightmares. Eight City/Fosse 'keepers have conceded double figures over the years, though not all while they were with the Foxes. The most unfortunate was Horace Bailey; the former Fosse stopper let in a dozen against – of all sides – Nottingham Forest, during the 1908/09 campaign. Three 'keepers have let in eleven, namely Tom DeVille (Fosse v. Rotherham Town), Alick Grant (Newport v. Notts County) and Jack Beby (Crystal Palace v. Exeter City) in 1891/92, 1948/49 and 1933/34 respectively. Bill Rowley let in ten while keeping goal for Stoke against Preston North End in 1899/90, while George Perkins let in a far from perfect ten for Fosse against Market Harboro in 1903/04. Joe Wright let in ten during a 10-2 loss by Torquay at the hands of Fulham, and last but not least, Sandy McLaren saw ten put past him for City v. Wolves in 1937/38.

KITTED OUT

Though City's kit has developed over the years, it hasn't changed dramatically or, unlike Cardiff City in 2013/14, completely beyond recognition! Leicester Fosse began with black shirts with a light blue sash, white shorts and black socks; this was worn from 1884 to 1886. For the next four years, Fosse's kit resembled Aston Villa's as a claret and blue shirt was adopted. In 1890, when white shirts and navy blue shorts became the colours of a club still searching for an identity. In 1899, finally, navy blue shirts, white shorts and blue socks were adopted for the first time – but yet again, it was short lived. Between 1901 and 1903, Fosse resembled something close to the current Uruguay kit with a few variations, until between 1903 and 1913 it was a return to navy shirts, white shorts and black socks. In 1913, the socks became navy blue as well. As Fosse's days were numbered and City emerged from the ashes, between 1915 and 1921, Foxes fans could be forgiven for thinking the club had changed its identity to that of Huddersfield Town! Striped blue-and-white shirts, white shorts and blue socks were worn until navy blue shirts and white shorts returned – and stayed – with a mixture of black or blue socks until 1946. From there on, it was blue socks until 1966 when, for three years, an all navy blue kit was used for the first time. In 1969/70, white socks were added – then ditched for navy blue for the next two years before a revolutionary all white kit with blue piping was used for one season in 1972/73. From 1973 to 1987, it was back to navy blue and white shorts and socks, with the occasional experimental stripes here and there and tinkering with the trims on shorts and jerseys. In 1987, red trim was added for the first time, and blue socks made a return from 1990 to 1992. From 1992 to 1996 was all blue again, then white shorts came back until 2002, and then it was all navy blue – again! From 2003 to 2007 white shorts came back, then

2007 to 2009 was all-blue before a return to blue shirts, white shorts and blue socks bring us bang up to date. In recent times, during each season there has been a tweak here and there, but these are City's traditional colours. Expect more variations in years to come!

KIT MANUFACTURERS

Staying with kits, these are the companies who have made the Foxes kits:

1976–1988	Admiral
1988–1990	Scoreline
1990–1992	Bukta
1992–2000	Fox Leisure
2000–2005	Le Coq Sportif
2005–2007	JJB
2007–2009	Jako
2009/2010	Joma
2010–2012	Burrda
2012–2014	Puma

ENGLISH HALL OF FAME MEMBERS

Five former Foxes have been inducted into the English Hall of Fame. The first two were legendary 'keepers Gordon Banks and Peter Shilton, who were inducted in the inaugural draft in 2002. A year later, Gary Lineker became the third City star to join the former greats, and a year later, Don Revie joined the ranks of the great and good – though as a manager rather than the player he was for the Foxes. The last legend to be inducted was Scotsman Frank McLintock – not sure how that works!

The list, as it stands, is:

2002	Gordon Banks	(inaugural inductee)
2002	Peter Shilton	(inaugural inductee)
2003	Gary Lineker	
2004	Don Revie	(inducted as a manager)
2009	Frank McLintock	

IS THERE A FIRE DRILL?

A League Cup second round replay between Brighton and Oldham Athletic in September 1977 unsurprisingly attracted thelowest-ever recorded crowd for a competitive fixture at Filbert Street. Just 1,840 hardy souls attended the midweek autumnal fixture with the league, in their infinite wisdom, deciding that, as the two teams couldn't be separated after draws at the Goldstone Ground and Boundary Park, a venue somewhere in the middle of the country would suffice for a third bite at the cherry. The Latics finally emerged triumphant, and even then after extra time, with a 2-1 win finally putting the tie to bed. At least the size of the gate ensured the match would never be forgotten!

BEST AND WORST XI?

The team nobody wants a place in – the 'Leicester Till I Die Worst City XI of All Time'. Voted by users of the alternative City fans' website, the eleven players who polled the most votes are:

Worst XI as voted for by LTID
Goalkeeper: Ricardo Pierira
Right-back: Robbie Neilson

Left-back: Ryan McGivern
Centre-back: Frank Sinclair
Centre-back: Franck Rolling
Right midfielder: Momo Sylla
Centre midfielder: Junior Lewis
Centre midfielder: Dennis Wise
Left midfielder: Alan Rogers
Striker: Ade Akinbiyi
Striker: Mark DeVries
Manager: Peter Taylor.

In contrast, the site also voted for the best-ever City XI – or the perfect team. Definitely the starting eleven every City player present and past would like to see their names in!

Best XI as voted for by LTID
Goalkeeper: Gordon Banks
Right-back: Adam Black
Left-back: David Nish
Centre-back: Matt Elliott
Centre-back: Steve Walsh
Right midfielder: David Gibson
Centre midfielder: Muzzy Izzet
Left midfielder: Keith Weller
Striker: Arthur Rowley
Striker: Gary Lineker
Striker: Frank Worthington
Manager: Martin O'Neill

WORLD CUP

A dozen City players have represented the club during the World Cup, with Gordon Banks also being World Cup winner.

Stretching back to 1954, there have been eight World Cups where no City player has been selected, while in 1958, 1986, 1990 and 2002, there were two Foxes involved. Goalkeeper John Anderson was the very first City player to travel to the World Cup in 1954 – albeit with Scotland, while Riyad Mahrez was the latest member of this exclusive club when he was selected by Algeria for Brazil 2014. The chosen twelve are:

1954	John Anderson
1958	Willie Cunningham
1958	Ken Leek
1966	Gordon Banks*
1982	John O'Neill
1986	John O'Neill
1986	Paul Ramsey
1990	Gary McAllister
1990	David Kelly
1998	Matt Elliott
1998	Kasey Keller
2002	Muzzy Izzet
2014	Riyad Mahrez

*Won the 1966 World Cup while at Leicester

FOX HUNTERS

Every team has a striker who always seems to score against them and the Foxes are no different. Below are ten players who City have not enjoyed facing over the years.

Dixie Dean managed eighteen goals against City, all while with Everton but is only our equal worst nemesis. George Brown notched nine for Huddersfield Town and the same amount for Aston Villa to stake a claim as the most feared hitman. Charlie Wyman scored goals against the Foxes for in every team he played for – ten for Southampton, five for Preston and two for Newcastle United to make it seventeen in total. Jimmy Dunne scored sixteen: eleven for Sheffield United, a couple for Arsenal and three for Southampton. Gordon Hodgson also totalled sixteen, with nine coming during a spell with Liverpool and another seven with Leeds United. Jimmy Greaves grabbed thirteen for Spurs and another couple for Chelsea to tot up fifteen goals against City. Dave Halliday spanned the breadth of the nation as he scored seven for Sunderland, four for Arsenal and three for Manchester City. Another legendary figure, Denis Law, scored fourteen in total, all while he was in Manchester – thirteen for United and one for the Blues. Ray Charnley scored all of his thirteen goals against the Foxes for Blackpool, and Graham Leggat achieved a similar feat in the colours of Fulham. Finally, Dennis Westcott scored eight for Wolves and five for Blackburn Rovers to tally up thirteen, and Jock Peddie bagged nine for Manchester United and another four for Newcastle to make it yet another unlucky thirteen!

UNLUCKY FOR SOME?

Unreliable crowd figures make the often-quoted record low crowd between Stockport County and City likely to be inaccurate – it was claimed just thirteen paying punters turned up to watch the game, but more accurate estimates place the crowd at close to 1,000. The lowest recorded gate therefore is the 1,327 hardy souls who turned up to see City take on Charlton Athletic in the Full Members' Cup in 1987. The game was played at Crystal Palace's Selhurst Park, while the FA Cup tie at Maidstone United attracted just 1,638 fans. The lowest home gate is 3,058 for an Anglo-Italian Cup tie against West Bromwich Albion – well, it was a preliminary round!

GORDON BANKS: QUOTE/UNQUOTE

Some pearls of wisdom and thoughts from the greatest City and England 'keeper of all-time.

That save from Pelé's header was the best I ever made. I didn't have any idea how famous it would become – to start with, I didn't even realise I'd made it at all.

On winning a first trophy with the Foxes:

We wanted to win it, and so did every other club. There was no putting the reserves out and stuff like that. That was my first winners' medal when we beat Stoke over two legs and winning it was a great feeling. We were winning games, growing in confidence and becoming better players.

On hearing he'd been called up for England for the first time:

I was down at the ground. We had this little room with a snooker table in it which we met up in once we had finished training. We were having a game of snooker when Matt Gillies came in. He came up to me, shook me by the hand and said: 'Congratulations, you're in the England team.' I couldn't quite believe it and I thought how does he know that when the squad haven't even assembled yet? Obviously Alf Ramsey must have said something to him. It came as something of a shock to me but also it was a great delight, obviously. I remember feeling very, very proud.

On the current England No. 1:

Joe Hart is our No. 1 and has been ever since the 2010 World Cup, and I personally wouldn't want anyone else in goal for us at this tournament. He has to say to himself: 'I got back into the team at Manchester City after being dropped, I had a decent season and won two trophies with my club and I'm in the England team and I have the chance to be a star of the World Cup here. For me, the others [Ben Foster and Fraser Forster] are good goalkeepers but Hart is by far and away the best in England at the minute and one of the best in the world.

1949 FA CUP

City first reached the FA Cup final in 1949 after more than sixty unsuccessful attempts in previous seasons. Birmingham City proved a difficult obstacle to get past in the third round with the first game at St Andrews ending 1-1 after extra time. It was the same outcome at Filbert Street where the teams once again were locked at 1-1 after extra time, but despite City losing the toss for the second replay, the Foxes won 2-1 back at St Andrews with more than 100,000 watching all three matches. A 2-0 home win over Preston North End proved an easier passage in round four, but the fifth round proved to be an incredible game at Kenilworth Road where City's clash with Luton Town ended 5-5 after extra time! The replay was no less entertaining, with City winning 5-3 in front of almost 40,000 fans. With Wembley in sight, Brentford were dispatched 2-0 at Griffin Park to set up a semi-final with Portsmouth at Highbury. More than 62,000 fans packed in Arsenal's home ground to see City create club history by beating Pompey 3-1 and earn a date with Wolves in the final.

Wolves, twice winners previously, started strong favourites against Division Two City, particularly as 'keeper Ian McGraw was ruled out with a broken finger and twenty-goal striker Don Revie was also injured. The bookies looked to have got it right, too, as Jessie Pye scored two first-half goals to put Wolves 2-0 up at the break. Mal Griffiths halved the deficit on 47 minutes, and Chisholm had a goal disallowed shortly after as the Foxes rallied. Sammy Smyth restored Wolves' two-goal advantage on 64 minutes and Wolves played out the remainder of the game to win 3-1.

The stats from the day:

FA Cup final, 30 April 1949

Leicester City   1–3   Wolverhampton Wanderers

Griffiths 47   Pye 13, 42

                            Smyth 64

Wembley Stadium, London

Attendance: 98,920

Referee: R. A. Mortimer (Huddersfield)

City: Gordon Bradley, Ted Jelly, Sandy Scott, Walter Harrison, Norman Plummer, Johnny King, Mal Griffiths, Jack Lee, Jimmy Harrison, Ken Chisholm, Charlie Adam.

Manager: Johnny Duncan

Wolves: Bert Williams, Roy Pritchard, Terry Springthorpe, Billy Crook, Bill Shorthouse, Billy Wright, Johnny Hancocks, Sammy Smyth, Jesse Pye, Jimmy Dunn, Jimmy Mullen.

Manager: Stan Cullis

SEEING RED

Notable dismissals in Foxes' history include Teddy King, who became the first City player ever to be sent for an early bath in 1919 – though he goes into the record books for City, Fosse had a player sent off some twenty-two years earlier. With that in mind, the first player at the club to receive his marching orders was Willie Freebairn, during a second tier clash at Lincoln City. Dion Dublin marked his City debut in August 2004 with a red card and became the first player to achieve the unwanted feat

– the game ended 0-0. Bob Pollock and Ike Evenson became the first Fosse players to be dismissed during the same game – a trip to Bolton Wanderers in 1905 and a game Fosse won 1-0! No City fan could ever think of red cards and not think of Foxes stalwart Steve Walsh, who was dismissed a club record nine times.

HE COMES FROM A LAND DOWN UNDER

Danny Tiatto arrived at City in 2004, with Ben Thatcher moving in the opposite direction to Manchester City. Tiatto soon had an army of new admirers with his no-holds-barred approach to the game matched by a never-say-die attitude. Crunching tackles were a regular part of his game and a number of red cards during his time in Manchester led to him agreeing to undergo a course of anger management – not that it seemed to work judging by one touchline altercation he had with Kevin Keegan, who ended up with his hands around Tiatto's throat! Tiatto walked off with the LCFC Player of the Year in 2004/05 – undoubtedly the highlight of his three-year stay at the Walkers, during which he made eighty-three appearances in all competitions, scoring three goals. In 2007, he returned to Australia to play for Queensland Roar before returning to one of his former clubs, Melbourne Knights, in 2010.

ROBBIE SAVAGE – A LEAGUE OF HIS OWN!

Robbie Savage – there really is only one Robbie! Whether it's quotes, incidents or awards, there is never a dull moment, so here's our selection of some of his best off-field moments – first a fact file on the man they nicknamed 'Mr Marmite':

Name: Robert William Savage
Years: 1997–2002
Born: Wrexham
Date of birth: 18 October 1974
Clubs: Manchester United, Crewe Alexandra, Leicester City, Birmingham City, Blackburn Rovers, Derby County, Brighton and Hove Albion
Debut: Aston Villa (h), 9 August 1987
Appearances: 189 + 15 as substitute
Goals: 9

Savage Said It

- 'Bolton started the game with an intendency.' Robbie invents a new word...

- 'Outside the box, that's a free-kick but inside the box, I don't think it's a penalty.' Just stating the obvious...

- 'You want to take your rose-scented glasses off, mate.' Robbie to a caller on his Radio 5 Live phone-in.

- 'Leicester were already relegated and I was on fourteen bookings so I could have said I didn't want to risk playing. I decided to play and give it my all and that's me. I love football and I will carry on giving 150 per cent.' Robbie booked in his final Foxes appearance and picking up a two-match ban for his new club Birmingham.

- 'I am not Pelé or Maradona...' No comment!

- 'I look at myself and read what people say on the Internet and some fans say the club should get rid of me, which shows how fickle some people can be.' Rams fans didn't always appreciate his style...

- 'Anybody can manage Wales. That's been proved.' The final nail in Robbie's international career?

- 'If he [Toshack] thinks there is lots of young Welsh talent coming through, then good luck to him.' The end of Robbie's international career is nigh...

- 'I'm not the best passer of a ball but I was pleased overall against Bolton.'
- 'I'm upset. There was nothing like pulling on the red shirt.' See above...
- 'John Toshack said it was my way or the highway —well I'm on the M56.' Robbie on his decision to quit international football with Wales.
- 'I was desperate to find a club at the time and I was pleading with Alan Birchenall to see if he could have a word on my behalf. I called Dickov too, and I was desperate to come back to City. I think Milan was up for it but Nigel Pearson said no. I think he thought my legs had gone. It certainly wasn't the money as Derby were going to pay 90 or 95 per cent of my wages, but they still said no. I suppose I can't blame Nigel. It was the right decision as he went on to take City straight back up to the Championship, but I did want to prove to him that I was not finished.' Robbie in 2009, sad his dream of returning to City never materialised.
- 'What Alan Hansen's done is unbelievable,' he says of the former Liverpool captain. 'He won loads of things, but not many players have done that. I have been an average Premier League player, and a Championship player, so I can speak for the majority of footballers. Not everybody's won Champions Leagues.' Robbie on his impending media career.
- Savage tweet number 1: 'This is commitment for you!! Lol smashed my huge nose on the camera!'
- Savage tweet number 2: '20 years as a footballer – 1 broken leg, 1 broken neck, 7 knee ops, 3 hernias. As a dancer – 5 weeks, a broken nose!' Both tweets relate to an injury sustained on Strictly Come Dancing, 2013.

Poohgate
In April 2004, Robbie took an impromptu trip to the referee's changing rooms where he (ahem) left a message in Graham

Poll's toilet! Here's how the incident – or the fall-out (apologies) – was dealt with. The BBC reported:

> Leicester have fined Robbie Savage two weeks' wages after he used the toilet in the referee's dressing room before Saturday's game with Aston Villa. The Welsh international entered referee Graham Poll's dressing room without permission.
>
> Poll reported Savage to the Football Association for breaking a rule which says a player cannot enter the referee's dressing room without permission. 'Robbie Savage has been fined the maximum permissible two weeks' wages,' said a Leicester spokesman.
>
> 'Leicester City were made aware of the incident on Saturday evening by match referee Graham Poll and then conducted their own investigation. The club has spoken with Robbie Savage and communicated the decision to him.'
>
> Savage could also face an improper conduct charge from the Football Association. A spokesman said: 'We can confirm we are examining the referee's report concerning an incident involving Robbie Savage.'

Robbie won an award in 2010 from the Plain English Campaign. He accepted the award saying,

> I'm completely overwhelmed. To think that a boy from Wrexham can win this award so early into my broadcasting career – it genuinely is a great honour. I love doing my radio work and know that I've still got an awful lot to learn. It's a good job it's for plain English. If it was for plain Welsh, I would have been struggling.

In the *Observer Sport Monthly* in November 2003, Robbie's shocking tumble for City *v.* Derby earned him a place in the all-time Worst Ever Dives Top 10. *The Observer* wrote:

Number 4: Robbie Savage

Derby *v.* Leicester, 15 September 2001

Robbie makes it so high in the list for sheer effort: a corrosive 90 minutes, a last-minute dive in the area, a hopeful look to the referee and a fist-pumping explosion in front of the home fans. Derby players chased him all the way to the corner flag, then tried to mug him in the tunnel afterwards.

'We've seen players for years who are very clever at diving for penalties,' said Derby boss Jim Smith. 'But he's not very clever and his penalties become riots. It's always him.'

Robbie said: 'I've never dived in my career. I was blameless.'

And finally, one more classic quote:

I love football, that's what people don't realise. They just see the hair and the teeth, the tan and the big house, the car and the clothes, and houses all over the world. What they don't see is that when I go home to the model wife, look over the golf course, go for a dip ... I watch ESPN, Spanish, German football, everything. Any league in the world, I watch it all the time. My knowledge of football is up there with the best and that's why I want to stay in it.'

Thank God he did...

LET THERE BE LIGHT

Like many clubs, City introduced floodlights for the first time in 1957, when the technology had been approved and quickly became a must-have addition to any stadium looking to increase their options. Night matches had long been a thing of fancy for most football fans but advances in construction and science made the illumination of darkened stadia one of the single-most important developments of football in England.

So, on 23 October 1957, the lights were switched on for the first time at Filbert Street for a midweek friendly with Borussia Dortmund – won by City by 1-0. Less than a month later, the lights were switched on for a League game against Preston North End with the winter darkness making visibility poor despite the match kicking off at 3 p.m.! The Lilywhites left with a 3-1 win, making the 27,000-plus crowd wonder if the floodlights were all they were cracked up to be! In March 1959, City took on Birmingham City for a first competitive game under the lights and a struggling Foxes side were again beaten, this time 4-2 by Blues.

LEAGUE CUP FOXES

City have a proud record in the League Cup, having reached the final five times. Here are the vital stats from all our final tie appearances:

1964 League Cup final
First Leg
15 April 1964
Stoke City   1–1   Leicester City
Bebbington   Gibson

Victoria Ground, Stoke
Attendance: 22,309
Referee: W. Clements
Stoke: Lawrie Leslie, Bill Asprey, Tony Allen, Calvin Palmer, George Kinnell, Eric Skeels, Peter Dobing, Dennis Viollet, John Ritchie, Jimmy McIlroy, Keith Bebbington.
Manager: Tony Waddington
Leicester City: Gordon Banks, John Sjoberg, Colin Appleton, Max Dougan, Ian King, Graham Cross, Howard Riley, Terry Heath, Ken

Keyworth, Dave Gibson, Mike Stringfellow.
Manager: Matt Gillies

Second Leg
22 April 1964
Leicester City   3–2   Stoke City
Stringfellow   Viollet
Gibson   Kinnell
Riley

Filbert Street, Leicester
Attendance: 25,372
Referee: A. Jobling
City win 4-3 on aggregate

1965 League Cup final
First leg
15 March 1965
Chelsea   3–2   Leicester City
Tambling 33   Appleton 46
Venables pen 70   Goodfellow 75
McCreadie 81

Stamford Bridge, London
Attendance: 20,690
Referee: Jim Finney (Hereford)
Chelsea: Peter Bonetti, Marvin Hinton, Ron Harris, John Hollins, Allan Young, John Boyle, Bert Murray, George Graham, Eddie McCreadie, Terry Venables, Bobby Tambling.
Manager: Tommy Docherty
City: Gordon Banks, John Sjoberg, Richard Norman, Len Chalmers, Ian King, Colin Appleton, Billy Hodgson, Graham Cross, Jimmy Goodfellow, David Gibson, Tom Sweenie.
Manager: Matt Gillies

Second leg
5 April 1965
Leicester City   0–0   Chelsea

Filbert Street, Leicester
Attendance: 26,957
Referee: Kevin Howley (Billingham)
City: Gordon Banks, Clive Walker, Richard Norman, Bobby Roberts, John Sjoberg, Colin Appleton, Billy Hodgson, Graham Cross, Jimmy Goodfellow, David Gibson, Mike Stringfellow.
Manager: Matt Gillies

1997 League Cup final
6 April 1997
Leicester City   1–1   Middlesbrough
Heskey 118   Ravanelli 95

Wembley Stadium, London
Attendance: 76,757
Referee: Martin Bodenham (Cornwall)
City: Kasey Keller, Simon Grayson, Mike Whitlow (Mark Robins 105), Steve Walsh, Pontus Kåmark, Spencer Prior, Muzzy Izzet (Scott Taylor 108), Neil Lennon, Garry Parker, Steve Claridge, Emile Heskey.
Manager: Martin O'Neill
Middlesbrough: Mark Schwarzer, Neil Cox, Curtis Fleming, Nigel Pearson, Gianluca Festa, Craig Hignett, Robbie Mustoe, Juninho, Emerson, Mikkel Beck, Fabrizio Ravanelli.
Manager: Bryan Robson

Replay
16 April 1997
Leicester City   1–0   Middlesbrough
Claridge 100

Hillsborough Stadium, Sheffield

Attendance: 39,428

Referee: Martin Bodenham (Cornwall)

City: Kasey Keller, Simon Grayson, Mike Whitlow (Jamie Lawrence 109), Steve Walsh, Pontus Kåmark, Spencer Prior, Muzzy Izzet, Neil Lennon, Garry Parker, Steve Claridge (Mark Robins 117), Emile Heskey.

Manager: Martin O'Neill

Middlesbrough: Ben Roberts, Neil Cox (Mikkel Beck 105), Valdimir Kinder, Nigel Pearson, Gianluca Festa (Steve Vickers 76), Craig Hignett (Alan Moore 105), Robbie Mustoe, Juninho, Emerson, Clayton Blackmore, Fabrizio Ravanelli.

Manager: Bryan Robson

1999 League Cup final

21 March 1999

Leicester City   0–1   Tottenham Hotspur
                          Nielsen 90

Wembley, London

Attendance: 77,892

Referee: Terry Heilbron (County Durham)

City: Kasey Keller, Matt Elliott, Steve Walsh, Gerry Taggart, Robert Ullathorne, Steve Guppy, Neil Lennon, Muzzy Izzet, Robbie Savage (Theodoros Zagorakis 90), Tony Cottee, Emile Heskey (Ian Marshall 74).

Manager: Martin O'Neill

Spurs: Ian Walker, Stephen Carr, Sol Campbell, Ramon Vega, Justin Edinburgh, Darren Anderton, Steffen Freund, Allan Nielsen, David Ginola (Andy Sinton 90), Les Ferdinand, Steffen Iversen.

Manager: George Graham

2000 League Cup final

27 February 2000

Leicester City   2–1   Tranmere Rovers
Elliott 29, 81   Kelly 77

Wembley Stadium, London
Attendance: 74,313
Referee: Alan Wilkie (Durham)
City: Tim Flowers, Frank Sinclair, Matt Elliott, Gerry Taggart, Steve
Guppy, Muzzy Izzet, Robbie Savage, Neil Lennon, Stefan Oakes
(Andy Impey 77), Emile Heskey, Tony Cottee (Ian Marhsall 89).
Manager: Martin O'Neill
Tranmere: Joe Murphy, Reuben Hazell, Dave Challinor, Clint Hill,
Gareth Roberts, Andy Parkinson (Steve Yates 66), Gary Jones, Nick
Henry, Alan Mahon, David Kelly, Scott Taylor.
Manager: John Aldridge

CITY IN EUROPE

City's European record may not be a source of great pride, but
at least the Foxes have competed at the highest level and, in
years to come, things will hopefully improve. The fact is, City
were in Europe long before many of the teams who went on
to dominate English and European football. After being beaten
in the 1961 FA Cup final by double-winning Tottenham, the
Foxes won entry into the 1961/62 European Cup Winners'
Cup competition. Spurs automatically went into the European
Cup, so their place in the ECWC was vacant and, by default or
not, City were delighted to have the opportunity. Of course, the
irony was that the Foxes drew Northern Ireland's Glentoran out
of the hat for the preliminary round – it was hardly a European
adventure, travelling to Windsor Park in Belfast! Still, there
was a job to do and Glentoran were comfortably dispatched
4-1, with goals from Jimmy Walsh (2), Colin Appleton and Ken
Keyworth settling the first leg. The return at Filbert Street was

a formality as City won 3-1 thanks to strikes from Gordon Wills, Hugh McIImoyle and Keyworth to complete a 7-2 aggregate victory.

Then followed a plum draw in round one as City were paired with Atlético Madrid. More than 25,000 fans turning out at Filbert Street to witness the first truly European night under the lights, and the Spaniards left with a valuable 1-1 draw with Keyworth on target for the Foxes. The second leg showed City's inexperience in playing on foreign soil as Atleti turned in a polished display to win 2-0 and progress to the next round with a 3-1 aggregate win.

The 1997 League Cup triumph by Martin O'Neill's City meant, after a thirty-six-year wait, the Foxes were back in Europe in the shape of the UEFA Cup. This time the first leg was in Madrid, too. Backed by 3,000 travelling fans, City took the lead after just 12 minutes, when Ian Marshall converted Steve Walsh's headed cross to give City a crucial away goal. It was a lead held until the 69th minute, when former Middlesbrough playmaker Juninho levelled and, three minutes later, the majority of the 35,000 crowd were celebrating again as Christian Vieri converted a hotly disputed penalty to give Atleti a slender 2-1 advantage. The second leg was a disappointment after such a spirited display, with City unable to find the goal that would put them in the driving seat and Atleti once again left Filbert Street with a victory having secured a 2-0 win.

More League Cup success in 2000 meant Peter Taylor's men could have another crack at European football, but yet again, City would fall at the first hurdle in the UEFA Cup . With a tie against one of European football's greatest names, Red Star Belgrade, the all-seater Filbert Street was packed to capacity for the visit of the Yugoslavians. City were a goal down within a minute as a 30-yard shot flew though smoke caused by flares and past Tim Flowers at speed. Gerry Taggart levelled and when Red Star were reduced to ten men, it looked as though the Foxes would go and win the first leg, but Stan Collymore was denied near the end by a superb save, and Red Star held out for a 1-1 draw. In a highly controversial second leg, played at the Gerhard Hanappi Stadium in Vienna, crowd trouble marred the game before, during and afterwards. Red Star were playing in Vienna due to the security risks of playing in Belgrade, but with 100,000 Serbs based in Austria, the atmosphere was hostile and unpleasant and several City players were racially abused during the game. The hosts drew first blood, but Muzzy Izzet levelled just before the break to restore parity. It was a brief respite, however, as Belgrade scored twice after the break to secure a 3-1 win and a 4-2 aggregate victory overall. City's time will come again, but in the meantime, the overall record is: Played 8, Won 2, Drawn2, Lost 4, For 11, Against 13. Top European scorer: Ken Keyworth (3).

SOUTH COAST HOLIDAYS?

City embarked on a tour of the south coast of England as part of their preseason plans for 1999/2000 campaign. It was not against many A-listers in world football, but it gave the opportunity for Foxes fans to make the 120-mile trip to watch the mini-tour that lasted six days in July and, when the sun shone, allowed the travelling support to top up their tan! The tour began with an entertaining 3-2 win over Bournemouth, with Arnar Gunnlaugsson, Emile Heskey and Kevin Campbell finding the net. Three days later and Dorset was swapped for Devon as the Foxes turned up at Plainmoor to face Torquay United – a dispiriting 2-1 defeat with Kevin Wilson scoring the City consolation. Four days later, the tour was completed in Hampshire as Portsmouth added more concern with a 2-1 win at Fratton Park. Matt Elliott scored City's goal in what was an underwhelming end to the trip.

ARTIFICIAL INTELLIGENCE

During the early 1980s, all-weather pitches – also called Astroturf or plastic pitches – were introduced by a number of clubs, much to the general chagrin of many players and supporters. The Foxes played in thirteen matches on the artificial mostrosities. It's fair to say that City, along with a lot of other clubs, never enjoyed playing on anything but grass, and the record proves as much with just one win and ten defeats from thirteen games played. The first four games were all against Queens Park Rangers from 1981 to 1985, and only a 2-2 draw in 1982/83 gave brief respite from the poor run. Luton and Oldham Athletic were the other two sides that City faced on plastic, but it was a 1-0 win at Loftus Road in 1986/87 that proved to be the Foxes' only victory.

The complete record is: Played 13, Won 1, Drawn 2, Lost 10, For 10, Against 27.

LEICESTER CITY FC PLAYERS OF THE YEAR

Here are the Foxes players who have been voted the best season performers by City fans from 1988 to 2014 – Robbie Savage is the only player to win in successive years. Gary Mills is the only other player to win the award twice, in 1990 and 1992.

1987/88	Steve Walsh
1988/89	Alan Paris
1989/90	Gary Mills
1990/91	Tony James
1991/92	Gary Mills
1992/93	Colin Hill
1993/94	Simon Grayson
1994/95	Kevin Poole

1995/96	Garry Parker
1996/97	Simon Grayson
1997/98	Matt Elliott
1998/99	Tony Cottee
1999/00	Gerry Taggart
2000/01	Robbie Savage
2001/02	Robbie Savage
2002/03	Paul Dickov
2003/04	Les Ferdinand
2004/05	Danny Tiatto
2005/06	Joey Guðjónsson
2006/07	Iain Hume
2007/08	Richard Stearman
2008/09	Steve Howard
2009/10	Jack Hobbs
2010/11	Richie Wellens
2011/12	Kasper Schmeichel
2012/13	Wes Morgan
2013/14	Danny Drinkwater

NORWEGIAN BLUE

City embarked on a brief postseason tour of Norway in 1976, during which Bob Lee and Frank Worthington were particularly effective. Beginning on 13 May against Mjondalen, City won 5-0 thanks to goals from Keith Weller, Worthington, Lee and Gould (2). Four days later were the fantastically named Odd and, again, City eased home in style winning 4-1, with Lee grabbing a hat-trick and Weller also on target again. Two days after that and the tiring Foxes legs still had enough to beat Molde 3-1, with Lee (2) and Worthington on target. Four days later, the tour was wrapped up with a 2-1 win over Ski, courtesy of Garland and Earle.

FA CUP 1960/61

City took eleven games to reach the 1961 FA Cup final, but despite the huge effort to get to Wembley, it would ultimately end in disappointment. The journey began with a 3-1 win over Oxford United in front of 25,501 Filbert Street fans, and the fourth round draw was also kind, pitting City against Bristol City. The Robins were giving a decent account of themselves, and by the break the score was still 0-0. But the incessant rain meant the match was abandoned due to a waterlogged pitch. The rearranged game was far more one-sided, with City winning 5-1 in front of a crowd of more than 27,000. A fifth-round trip to St Andrews to face Birmingham resulted in a 1-1 draw. A huge crowd of 53,589 watched the match, and close to 42,000 watched the return at Filbert Street as Kenny Leek's brace secured a 2-1 win and a place in the last eight. Barnsley were next up and the South Yorkshire side proved dogged opponents, earning a 0-0 draw and winning a replay at Oakwell, but City would edge the game 2-1 after extra time. It's fascinating that, combining the two gates, almost 80,000 people watched the quarter-final tie. Next up were Sheffield United in the semi-final, but it would take three matches, each at a different venue, to settle the it. Played over ten days and watched by a combined audience of more than 130,000 fans, the first two clashes proved how evenly matched the teams were. The first game at Elland Road ended 0-0 and the replay at Nottingham Forest's City Ground also ended goalless. Finally, at St Andrews, City blunted the Blades with Leek, scoring his seventh of the competition and Jimmy Walsh grabbed the other.

Unfortunately, in Spurs, the Foxes met a team on a mission, and though neither team had scored by the hour mark (this despite City losing Len Chalmers with a broken leg just 20 minutes in and being reduced to ten men for the remainder of the game), the North Londoners finally broke the deadlock after 66 minutes and added a second 9 minutes later to end the game as a contest. Brave City had gave it their all, but Spurs had been driven by the prospect of wining the coveted League and Cup double and became the first side in sixty-four years to do so. The stats from the day are:

FA Cup final
6 May 1961
Tottenham Hotspur   2–0   Leicester City
Smith 66
Dyson 75

Wembley, London
Attendance: 100,000
Referee: J. Kelly
Tottenham Hotspur: Bill Brown, Peter Baker, Ron Henry, Danny Blanchflower, Maurice Norman, Dave Mackay, Cliff Jones, John White, Bobby Smith, Les Allen, Terry Dyson.
Manager: Bill Nicholson
City: Gordon Banks, Len Chalmers, Richie Norman, Frank McLintock, Ian King, Colin Appleton, Howard Riley, Jimmy Walsh, Hughie McIlmoyle, Ken Keyworth, Albert Cheesebrough.
Manager: Matt Gillies

GREAT SCOTS!

Scottish Premier League champions Aberdeen were the invited guests to take part in City's centenary match at Filbert Street in 1984. Under the tutelage of manager Alex Ferguson, the Dons had won the European Cup Winners' Cup in 1983, broken the dominance of Celtic and Rangers by securing the SPL title in 1980 and 1984, and won the Scottish Cup three times. They were arguably one of the best teams in Europe at that time, the perfect opposition in the high-profile friendly at Filbert Street. The game ended 1-1, with Steve Lynex converting from the penalty spot. Just five days earlier, City had travelled to Glasgow to draw 2-2 with Rangers at Ibrox, with goals from Gary Lineker and John O'Neill. In fact, playing Scottish teams at that time was not uncommon; City had three friendlies north of the border the previous season. City beat Inverness Caledonian Thistle 2-1 in March 1983, then Hearts 3-2 at Tynecastle in August 1983, and followed that with a 2-1 win over St Johnstone two days later. Lineker clearly enjoyed playing Scots teams as he found the net on all three matches.

BANKS INTEREST

City took part in a Gordon Banks benefit match on 19 April 1995. The Foxes faced an International XI with the crowd well and truly entertained following a 6-6 draw. David Speedie bagged a hat-trick, Mark Robins scored twice and Iwan Roberts once.

MASCOT GRAND NATIONAL

Alas, Filbert Fox has never troubled the winner's podium at the annual Mascot Grand National. First held at Huntingdon Racecourse in 1999, when seventeen mascots raced over 220 yards and six hurdles, Birmingham City's Beau Brummie Bear won the inaugural event. By 2000, numbers had swelled to forty-nine mascots with Watford's Harry the Hornet taking the crown. There was controversy in 2001 when Freddie the Fox (no direct relation, but a distant cousin) cantered home way ahead of everyone else – only to be unmasked as an Olympic athlete and disqualified! The race has since moved to Kempton and though Filbert still awaits his moment in the sun, he won't be giving up on his dream anytime soon.

List of winners

1999	Beau Brummie Bulldog – Birmingham City FC
2000	Harry the Hornet – Watford FC
2001	Dazzler the Lion – Rushden & Diamonds FC
2002	Chaddy the Owl – Oldham Athletic AFC
2003	Chaddy the Owl – Oldham Athletic AFC
2004	Graham the Gorilla – Finedon Volta FC
2005	Scoop Six Squirrel – *The Sun* newspaper
2006	Mickey the Monkey – Kick 4 Life
2007	Wacky Macky Bear – Saffron Walden Town FC
2008	Wacky Macky Bear – Saffron Walden Town FC
2009	Stag – Huntingdon Rugby Club
2010	Mr Bumble – Barnet FC
2011	not held
2012	Mr Bumble – Barnet FC
2013	Barry Barratt – Barratt Homes safety mascot

CHRISTMAS CRACKERS?

Hard as it may be to believe, league matches used to take place on Christmas Day. The fixture was finally abolished in 1958 as sense finally prevailed, but it had been in effect since 1894 when Bury dished out a 4-1 defeat in Greater Manchester – a year before the Shakers moved to Gigg Lane. The Foxes bounced back in style, winning nine and drawing four of the next thirteen Christmas Day fixtures, until the run ended with defeat to Blackpool in 1913. Though City enjoyed more success than disappointment on this day, just two wins from the final nine festive games suggested the time to finish couldn't come too soon. The final match was a 5-1 defeat away to Blackpool at Bloomfield Road in 1957. That said, the Foxes' overall record is actually quite good, having lost just thirteen of the forty-two games played and averaging more than two goals per game. The complete record is: Played 42, Won 22, Drawn 7, Lost 13, For 95, Against 56.

DAD'S ARMY

The City side that took to the field against Burnley on 18 September 2004 was the oldest in club history, with an average age of thirty-one years and 109 days. Ten players used were over thirty years of age, just three were in their twenties. The old boys held their own, too, drawing 0-0 with the Clarets to prove there's many a good tune played on an old fiddle!

UNUSUAL MIDDLE NAMES...

Emile Heskey has perhaps the best middle name of all City's players past and present, with the unforgettable 'Ivanhoe' literally in a league of its own. Stanley Victor Collymore is a decent name, as is William Risk Corbett, while Shirley Hubbard didn't really need a middle name...

THIS IS ENGLAND

England under-21s have made three appearances at Filbert Street over the years and never conceded a goal. In November 1979, England thrashed Bulgaria 5-0 in front of a disappointing 5,758 fans, but it would be another fifteen years before the

Under-21s returned to the Foxes' home. A 0-0 draw with Portugal in 1994 attracted a slightly better crowd, with 6,487 people in attendance. In 2001, the final game was played by the second most important England team, and 10,000 people watched the under-21s beat their Mexican counterparts 3-0.

(NOT-SO) INSTANT REPLAY

City had an unusual part to play in the longest-running FA Cup tie of the 1970s, though the Foxes weren't actively involved. As the FA Cup tie between Sheffield Wednesday and Arsenal dragged on, Filbert Street became a key part in a game that captured the imagination of the nation in a curious way. After games at Hillsborough and Highbury failed to separate the Owls and the Gunners, City's home ground was chosen as the neutral venue to finally settle the tie – or so we thought! The second replay in 15 January 1979 ended in an entertaining 2-2 draw in front of 25,011 fans. The third replay – and fourth meeting between the clubs – was played just three days later and was even better than the previous clash as the teams ended up sharing six goals in a 3-3 thriller at Filbert Street. The gate was understandably lower with just 17,008 fans attending as the marathon began to drain pockets as well as enthusiasm! The third meeting in Leicester finally settled the tie – at the fifth time of asking. Arsenal emerged victorious as they finally saw off Wednesday with a 2-0 victory in front of a very healthy 30,275. The spin-off for City was the extra revenue the matches generated, with 72,294 fans coming through the turnstiles in little over a week. Then there were the beers, the pies, the programmes – what a pity penalty shoot-outs were brought in! As for the Gunners, the effort was well worth it as Arsenal beat Manchester United 3-2 in the final at Wembley to crown one of the most epic Cup campaigns in living memory.

FOREST FIRE

Few matches get the pulse racing like a City *v.* Forest derby.
The fixture is 113 years old and has seen some tempestuous
clashes over the years. The Foxes are just edging the battle by
forty wins to thirty-nine. Here is the complete record against
our East Midlands rivals:

Championship

19 February 2014	Nottingham Forest 2-2 Leicester City
9 November 2013	Leicester City 0-2 Nottingham Forest
4 May 2013	Nottingham Forest 2-3 Leicester City
10 November 2012	Leicester City 2-2 Nottingham Forest
27 March 2012	Leicester City 0-0 Nottingham Forest
20 October 2011	Nottingham Forest 2-2 Leicester City
22 April 2011	Nottingham Forest 3-2 Leicester City
29 November 2010	Leicester City 1-0 Nottingham Forest
27 February 2010	Leicester City 3-0 Nottingham Forest
5 December 2009	Nottingham Forest 5-1 Leicester City
5 March 2005	Leicester City 0-1 Nottingham Forest
17 December 2004	Nottingham Forest 1-1 Leicester City

English Division One

8 April 2003	Leicester City 1-0 Nottingham Forest
15 October 2002	Nottingham Forest 2-2 Leicester City

English Premier League

16 May 1999	Nottingham Forest 1-0 Leicester City
12 December 1998	Leicester City 3-1 Nottingham Forest
28 December 1996	Leicester City 2-2 Nottingham Forest
7 September 1996	Nottingham Forest 0-0 Leicester City
11 March 1995	Leicester City 2-4 Nottingham Forest
27 October 1994	Nottingham Forest 1-0 Leicester City

English Division One

06 February 1994	Nottingham Forest 4-0 Leicester City
24 October 1993	Leicester City 1-0 Nottingham Forest

English Division One (old)

22 March 1987	Nottingham Forest 2-1 Leicester City
11 October 1986	Leicester City 3-1 Nottingham Forest
22 March 1986	Nottingham Forest 4-3 Leicester City
8 September 1985	Leicester City 0-3 Nottingham Forest
27 April 1985	Leicester City 1-0 Nottingham Forest
25 November 1984	Nottingham Forest 2-1 Leicester City
5 May 1984	Leicester City 2-1 Nottingham Forest
4 December 1983	Nottingham Forest 3-2 Leicester City
28 February 1981	Leicester City 1-1 Nottingham Forest
20 September 1980	Nottingham Forest 5-0 Leicester City
14 March 1978	Nottingham Forest 1-0 Leicester City
24 September 1977	Leicester City 0-3 Nottingham Forest
22 January 1972	Nottingham Forest 1-2 Leicester City
18 October 1971	Leicester City 2-1 Nottingham Forest
18 January 1969	Nottingham Forest 0-0 Leicester City
9 November 1968	Leicester City 2-2 Nottingham Forest
4 May 1968	Leicester City 4-2 Nottingham Forest
19 March 1968	Nottingham Forest 2-1 Leicester City
25 February 1967	Nottingham Forest 1-0 Leicester City
8 October 1966	Leicester City 3-0 Nottingham Forest
30 April 1966	Leicester City 2-1 Nottingham Forest
4 December 1965	Nottingham Forest 2-0 Leicester City
27 February 1965	Nottingham Forest 2-1 Leicester City
17 October 1964	Leicester City 3-2 Nottingham Forest
29 February 1964	Leicester City 1-1 Nottingham Forest
8 October 1963	Nottingham Forest 2-0 Leicester City
19 February 1963	Nottingham Forest 0-2 Leicester City
25 October 1962	Leicester City 2-1 Nottingham Forest
28 April 1962	Leicester City 2-1 Nottingham Forest

9 December 1961	Nottingham Forest 0-0 Leicester City
22 April 1961	Nottingham Forest 2-2 Leicester City
3 December 1960	Leicester City 1-1 Nottingham Forest
2 April 1960	Leicester City 0-1 Nottingham Forest
14 November 1959	Nottingham Forest 1-0 Leicester City
18 April 1959	Nottingham Forest 1-4 Leicester City
29 November 1958	Leicester City 0-3 Nottingham Forest
1 March 1958	Nottingham Forest 3-1 Leicester City
19 October 1957	Leicester City 3-1 Nottingham Forest

English Division Two (old)

30 March 1957	Nottingham Forest 1-2 Leicester City
17 November 1956	Leicester City 0-0 Nottingham Forest
31 October 1955	Nottingham Forest 2-0 Leicester City
22 October 1955	Leicester City 5-2 Nottingham Forest
23 January 1954	Nottingham Forest 3-1 Leicester City
12 September 1953	Leicester City 1-0 Nottingham Forest
28 February 1953	Leicester City 1-1 Nottingham Forest
11 October 1952	Nottingham Forest 1-3 Leicester City
5 January 1952	Leicester City 3-1 Nottingham Forest
8 September 1951	Nottingham Forest 2-2 Leicester City
9 April 1949	Nottingham Forest 2-1 Leicester City
13 November 1948	Leicester City 4-2 Nottingham Forest
28 February 1948	Nottingham Forest 1-0 Leicester City
11 October 1947	Leicester City 3-1 Nottingham Forest
1 March 1947	Leicester City 1-1 Nottingham Forest
26 October 1946	Nottingham Forest 2-0 Leicester City
24 April 1937	Leicester City 2-1 Nottingham Forest
19 December 1936	Nottingham Forest 0-3 Leicester City
30 January 1936	Nottingham Forest 0-1 Leicester City
21 September 1935	Leicester City 2-1 Nottingham Forest
15 October 1921	Nottingham Forest 0-0 Leicester City
8 October 1921	Leicester City 2-2 Nottingham Forest
19 February 1921	Leicester City 2-0 Nottingham Forest

12 February 1921	Nottingham Forest 1-2 Leicester City
13 March 1920	Leicester City 0-0 Nottingham Forest
6 March 1920	Nottingham Forest 0-0 Leicester City
20 February 1915	Nottingham Forest 1-3 Leicester City
17 October 1914	Leicester City 3-1 Nottingham Forest
11 September 1913	Leicester City 5-1 Nottingham Forest
3 September 1913	Nottingham Forest 1-3 Leicester City
28 December 1912	Nottingham Forest 4-2 Leicester City
7 September 1912	Leicester City 3-1 Nottingham Forest
29 February 1912	Leicester City 1-1 Nottingham Forest
16 September 1911	Nottingham Forest 4-1 Leicester City

English Division One (old)

21 April 1909	Nottingham Forest 12-0 Leicester City
7 November 1908	Leicester City 0-3 Nottingham Forest

English Division Two (old)

20 April 1907	Leicester City 1-2 Nottingham Forest
15 December 1906	Nottingham Forest 2-1 Leicester City

Cup Results
FA Cup

17 January 2012   Leicester City 4-0 Nottingham Forest
(round three replay)
7 January 2012   Nottingham Forest 0-0 Leicester City
(round three)
9 February 1901   Nottingham Forest 5-1 Leicester City
(round one)

League Cup

18 September 2007 Nottingham Forest 2-3 Leicester City
(round two)
14 December 1988 Nottingham Forest 2-1 Leicester City
(round four replay)

30 November 1988 Leicester City 0-0 Nottingham Forest
(round four)

Zenith Data Systems Cup
12 February 1992   Leicester City 1-1 Nottingham Forest
(Northern Area final first leg)
26 February 1992   Nottingham Forest 2-0 Leicester City
(Northern Area final second leg)   Forest won 3-1 on agg

Complete Record
Played 106, Won 40, Drawn 27, Lost 39, For 154, Against 167

CHARITY BEGINS AT HOME

The only time City have competed in the FA Charity Shield
(FA Community Shield these days) was back in 1970/71. The
Foxes earned a place in the final by default. As winners of the
second division, the Foxes were invited to contest the game,
which is traditionally between the Division One champions
(Premier League today). Arsenal, who had completed the
League and FA Cup double had declined the chance to play the
game and neither City or Liverpool, who had ended up runners-
up in the FA Cup, contested the game by right. Liverpool had
finished runners-up in the League, so the game was treated
with little respect by the Gunners and left to others to contest.
The Foxes hosted the game at Filbert Street in front of a sun-
drenched crowd of 25,104 and settled by a 15th-minute Steve
Whitworth tap-in. The 1-0 win over Bill Shankly's side remains
City's only FA Charity/Community Shield success to date.

INDIAN SUMMER

India took on Bangladesh in an experimental full international at Filbert Street in August 2000. But the Asian community largely ignored the game, edged 1-0 by India with only 2,588 fans bothering to come and watch. The fixture has not been repeated.

IZZET SAID IT...

Muzzy Izzet was one of the most popular City players of recent times – here's some of the things he's said about the Foxes.
On joining City:

I told manager Glenn Hoddle that it was maybe time to move. A week later he told me that Leicester wanted me on loan. The strange thing was I had no idea Martin O'Neill was looking at me. I didn't even meet him until I started training.

He told me he'd been watching me for a couple of years and I was the type of player he needed. I didn't know who Martin O'Neill was to be perfectly honest. I didn't know much about Leicester either.

On his debut as the City fans turned on O'Neill:

When I made my Leicester debut against Sheffield United I felt it was the biggest day of my life, because it was the day when I actually felt I'd become a professional footballer. For the first time I was playing in front of a big crowd. Even though they weren't happy, I tried to enjoy it.

On reaching Wembley so quickly:

That's how crazy football is. Two-and-half months after I'd been playing in front of two men and a dog, I'm playing against Crystal

Palace in front of 80,000 at Wembley. Bonkers! It was another great day.

On reported interest from Blackburn Rovers boss Graeme Souness:

I was very flattered that he was interested. I just felt that because it's my last year and with everything that's gone on here - I've come this far. Whatever happens at the end of this season, if I go or stay, I can say I stayed in January and did everything I could.

On putting City first:

That was the reason – I had come this far and it didn't feel right to walk out now. If I'd gone up to Blackburn and Leicester had gone down then questions would have been asked. 'Oh, he left,' they'd say. If I'm ever going to leave, then I don't want it to be on them terms. I've had such good times here. Because I went into the First Division with them I think I showed people here that's it's not just fun and games, I am actually serious about Leicester City. I could have gone elsewhere and got a four-year contract.

On being the subject of constant transfer gossip:

It's been a long while. I've been linked with other clubs before, but I just got to a stage where I was happy here. Now the only disappointment is that we're struggling as a football team and that's been hard. But who knows what's to come? That's the way I'm looking at it. I think the club know that if we go down then obviously I've got to look at things. I went into the First Division once with Leicester and we came straight back up, but with this being my last year then, if we go down, I would imagine the contract they will offer me to stay isn't going to be a Premier League contract.

On Robbie Savage:

I got on well with Sav. But I agree he is one of those players you love at your team but not when he's playing against you. He has done really well for himself wherever he has played and he looks to have a future media career ahead of him. But what people don't realise with Sav is he's a very insecure person and the brashness you know him for is his way of hiding this fact. But I think he's a top bloke.

On being selected to play for Turkey at the 2000 World Cup:

I'm just pleased I've made the decision and proud to be here with the lads. To be honest, I'd already made up my mind before Turkey asked me. Every player wants to perform on the big stage and I'm grateful for the opportunity. But I am half-Turkish. I've always felt that way. We used to go to a lot of Turkish weddings and sünnets – and things like that. Sünnets are a Muslim thing where you get circumcised and they hold a massive party for you. I had one when I was a little kid. So I've always been used to Turkish food and music and so on. It's part of the culture in our family.

On relegation from the Premier League in 2003/04:

I love this place – it's just a shame that we couldn't stay up because you never know, I might have been here for longer.

On his time with City:

Wow, it was like a roller coaster. Within ten games of my arriving we were at Wembley and looking forward to Premiership football. There was always something happening, a Cup final, Europe, they really were fantastic times. The end of course wasn't so happy, but I like to remember the early days.

1963 FA CUP FINAL

City had still been suffering from an FA Cup final hangover when they crashed out 5-2 to Stoke City at the first hurdle the season after the 1961 defeat to Spurs. Determined to give it another go, the Foxes began their quest for Wembley in 1963 with a comfortable 3-1 win at Grimsby Town in the third round, this was followed by a 3-1 home win over Ipswich Town at Filbert Street. Kenny Keyworth continued his run of a goal in each round by scoring the only goal in a 1-0 win over Leyton Orient at Brisbane Road. Now in the last eight, City were determined to go all the way to Wembley once more. A third away draw out of four didn't disrupt the run, with City beating Norwich 2-0 at Carrow Road, meaning only Liverpool stood between the Foxes and the final. Having already beaten the Reds home and away that season, City, pushing for the Division One title and sniffing the Holy Grail of a possible League and Cup double, travelled Hillsborough in high spirits. They were ahead after 18 minutes, when Mike Stringfellow opened the scoring. Roared on by half of the 65,000 crowd, City defended like lions and Gordon Banks was at his breathtaking best as the Foxes held on for a 1-0 victory. But that's when things began to go wrong as City's season began to fall apart, losing all four remaining League games to finish fourth. The poor form continued into the final where City were second best, going down disappointingly 3-1 to Manchester United. There was to be no third time lucky for the Foxes, who had now lost three finals in fourteen years. The stats for the final:

FA Cup final, 25 May 1963

Leicester City	1–3	Manchester United
Keyworth 80		Law 30
		Herd 57, 85

Wembley Stadium, London
Attendance: 99,604
Referee: Ken Aston
City: Gordon Banks, John Sjoberg, Richie Norman, Frank McLintock, Ian King, Colin Appleton, Howard Riley, Graham Cross, Ken Keyworth, Dave Gibson, Mike Stringfellow
Manager: Matt Gillies
Man United: David Gaskell, Tony Dunne, Noel Cantwell, Pat Crerand, Bill Foulkes, Maurice Setters, Johnny Giles, Albert Quixall, David Herd, Denis Law, Bobby Charlton
Manager: Matt Busby

CROSS PURPOSES?

Graham Cross has much to be proud of. Not only is he City's record appearance holder, but, like one of those kids at school who is good at every sport (and you secretly hate them), he was also an excellent cricketer, representing Leicestershire between 1961 and 1977. Football first, though, and Cross came close to notching 600 appearances for City, agonisingly finishing on 599. An inside-forward to begin with, he also played in central defence and as a wing-back for City between 1961 and 1975. He also holds the record for England under-23 appearances – winning ten caps and scoring one goal between 1963 and 1963 – though he never won a full cap for the national team.

Cross' talents were such that he could have easily swapped football for cricket but, as he chose the former for a career, he only played when he could for Leicestershire. He played eighty-three first class matches, scoring 2,079 runs (an average of 18.39), and scored eight half-centuries with a high score of seventy-eight. He also managed 61 catches and took an impressive ninety-two wickets – a proper all-rounder in more than one way.

A true City great, he excelled on the football and cricket pitch, and who knows how high he may have gone had he concentrated on just one sport?

WHIPPERSNAPPER!

City's youngest-ever debutant, aged only fifteen years and 203 days, is Ashley Chambers, who made his debut as a substitute against Blackpool on 15 September 2005. City won the game 2-1. Chambers would go on to make a further eight appearances for the Foxes, spending time on loan at Wycombe, Grimsby Town and York, before making the move to York permanent. He may not have set the world on fire at the Walkers Stadium, but he certainly made his mark.

SOMETHING OLD...

Had Kevin Phillips arrived at City a month later than he did, he would have almost certainly written his name into the club's record books as the oldest player to play for the club. When he retired on 3 May 2014, he was still thirty-two days shy of the record held by Joe Calvert, who was forty years and 313 days old when he played against Southampton on 13 December 1947 (just over a month older than Phillips). At least Phillips could claim to be the oldest debutant when made his bow against Leeds United on 18 January 2014, aged forty years 177 days. Phillips retired after the game against Doncaster on 3 May 2014, where he came on as a second-half substitute and received a standing ovation from both City and Rovers supporters in recognition of a magnificent career.

GIVE IT SOME WALL!

When Mark Wallington took his place between the sticks for the Division One match against Everton on 11 January 1975, little did he realise he was about to embark on a run that would earn him a place in the record books. Wallington wouldn't miss a League game for more than seven years, clocking up 331 consecutive league appearances until 9 March 1982, when he missed the 4-1 defeat at Stamford Bridge against Chelsea. He then clocked up another fifty-four appearances before eventually moving on in July 1985, having clocked up 460 appearances in all for the Foxes.

IT'S AN HONOUR...

Here is a chronological list of Foxes' honours. City have ended up runners-up nine times in various competitions over the years.

Honour	Position	Year
Division Two	Runners-up	1907/08
Division Two	Champions	1924/25
Division One	Runners-up	1928/29
Division Two	Champions	1936/37
FA Cup	Runners-up	1949
Division Two	Champions	1953/54
Division Two	Champions	1956/57
FA Cup	Runners-up	1961
FA Cup	Runners-up	1963
Football League Cup	Winners	1964
Football League Cup	Runners-up	1965
FA Cup	Runners-up	1969
Division Two	Champions	1970/71
FA Charity Shield	Winner	1971

Division Two	Champions	1979/80
Football League Cup	Winners	1997
Football League Cup	Runners-up	1999
Football League Cup	Winners	2000
Division One	Runners-up	2002/03
League One	Champions	2008/09
Championship	Champions	2013/14

PASTA MASTERS: THE STORY OF THE ANGLO-ITALIAN CUP

The Foxes entered the Anglo-Italian Cup in 1972, held at the end of the 1971/72 campaign. A 1-0 defeat to Calgari was followed by a 5-3 defeat to Atalanta in the Italian section of the competition. Back at Filbert Street, the Foxes got their revenge by beating Calgari 2-1 and then thrashing Atalanta 6-0 in front of 10,949 fans at Filbert Street. Sadly, despite goals meaning points, the Foxes just missed the cut and that was the end of the journey for that season. The facts and figures for 1971/72 are:

First Round
1 June 1972
Group 2

| Cagliari | 1-0 | Leicester |
| Atalanta | 3-2 | Sunderland |

Second Round
4 June 1972
Group 2

| Cagliari | 1-3 | Sunderland |
| Atalanta | 5-3 | Leicester |

Third Round
7 June 1972
Group 2
Leicester   2-1   Cagliari
Sunderland 0-0   Atalanta

Fourth Round
10 June 1972
Group 2
Sunderland 3-3   Cagliari
Leicester   6-0   Atalanta

Italian Ranking	P	W	D	L	GF	GA	Pts	Total
1. Roma	4	2	1	1	9	7	5	14
2. Atalanta	4	2	1	1	8	11	5	13
3. Cagliari	4	1	1	2	6	8	3	9
4. Sampdoria	4	1	0	3	3	9	2	5
5. Lanerossi Vicenza	4	0	1	3	3	17	1	4
6. Catanzaro	4	0	0	4	1	10	0	1

English Ranking	P	W	D	L	GF	GA	Pts	Total
1. Blackpool	4	4	0	0	18	1	8	26
2. Carlisle United	4	3	1	0	11	6	7	18
3. Leicester City	4	2	0	2	11	7	4	15
4. Birmingham City	4	2	1	1	8	5	5	13
5. Sunderland	4	1	2	1	8	7	4	12
6. Stoke City	4	2	0	2	6	4	4	10

NB: teams classified according to sum of points and goals scored.

Final
24 June 1972
Roma
Roma   3-1   Blackpool

The Foxes returned to the competition in 1992/93 and got off to a flyer with a 4-0 win over Grimsby Town (not the most Italian of opponents), but then lost 4-0 away to Newcastle United, ending the Foxes' interest. With poor crowds – just 4,112 for the game against Grimsby – City gave the much-maligned competition one more go in 1993/94, but a 4-3 defeat to Peterborough at London Road and a dull 0-0 draw with West Brom at Filbert Street in front of a paltry 3,588 fans not only meant another early exit, but also that the Foxes would never bother with the competition ever again (it would end two years later).

The complete record is: Played 8, Won 3, Drawn 2, Lost 5, For 18, Against 15.

SUPER SUBS

There have been various notable milestones set from the subs bench for City over the years. Subs weren't introduced until the 1965/66 season, and even then they were for injuries only in League games. The following season one sub was also allowed for Cup matches as well, but it was a long time before more than one sub was allowed on the bench when. In 1986/87, two were allowed during a game – one being a 'keeper – and in 1993/94, two could be chosen from three subs. The final increase (to date) was in 1995/96, when three subs could be used during a game, initially from three subs, but increased to five a year later and in 2009, that became seven – hence the bigger benches!

City's first sub was Jimmy Goodfellow, who replaced Graham Cross at home to Liverpool. Paul Matthews was the first League Cup sub in 1966, and Len Glover was the first FA Cup sub. Our first goalscoring sub was Tom Sweenie in April 1966 *v.* Blackburn Rovers, and a notable landmark of 100 goals by subs was reached when Craig Hignett scored against Arsenal in 2003. Steve Thompson, Martyn Waghorn, Paul Groves, Graham Fenton and Dany N'Guessan all made the debut from the bench for the Foxes and marked the occasion with a goal. The player with the most splinters in his backside from warming the bench so often is Trevor Benjamin, who came on fifty-four times as a sub while Jon Stevenson was used fourteen times as an extra man but never made a start.

ACCRINGTON STANLEY – WHO ARE THEY?

The Foxes have only played the team with arguably the most northern-sounding name in league football on one occasion. City beat Accrington Stanley 1-0 in the Carling Cup in August 2007, with James Wesolowski scoring the only goal of the game in East Lancashire. The teams have never met competitively in the League.

FOUR BY FOUR

The Foxes have shared eight goals on (fittingly) four separate occasions. The first 4-4 draw came away to Arsenal in 1961, and the second was also on a trip south when City held Southampton to a 4-4 draw at The Dell in 1967. It was twenty-eight years before the same scoreline reappeared, this time in an entertaining derby with Aston Villa at Villa Park, and the last eight-goal thriller was at White Hart Lane against Spurs in 2004.

The games and dates:

29 October 1961   *v.* Arsenal 4
14 January 1967   *v.* Southampton 4

22 February 1995   *v.* Aston Villa 4
22 February 2004   *v.* Tottenham Hotspur 4

THE PERFECT TEN

City's biggest-ever League victory was against Portsmouth in 1928 when the Foxes went goal crazy, beating Pompey 10-0. Ernie Hine scored a hat-trick, Len Barry got one, and a double hat-trick from Arthur Chandler (who else?) accounted for the goals that day. The return at Fratton Park was slightly less enjoyable, with Portsmouth exacting revenge and regaining their pride with a 1-0 home win.

STICKY TOFFEES

For pure entertainment and value for money, Leicester City *v.* Everton was the fixture of the season during the 1929/30 campaign. The Foxes left Goodison Park having edged a thrilling contest 5-4, but the return game was equally exciting as City repeated the feat, winning 5-4 again to make it a total of eighteen goals scored between the teams that season.

SIX AND THE CITY

After numerous high-scoring games during the 1929/30 campaign, the penultimate game of the season proved to be the best of the lot. It isn't often you score six goals and don't win – but then again it's almost unheard of that you could concede six goals but don't lose! That's exactly what City and Arsenal fans witnessed at Filbert Street in April 1930 as the Gunners headed back to North London having secured a 6-6 draw. The teams had also drawn just four days earlier, though this time it was a more conservative 1-1 score.

MEN AT THE TOP

These are the men who have managed Leicester City FC over the years:

Dates	Name	Notes
1884–1892	Ernest Marson	
1892–1894	George Johnson	
1894/1895	J. Lee	
1895–1897	Henry Jackson	
1897/1898	William Clark	
1898–1912	George Johnson	
1912–1914	John W. Bartlett	
1914/1915	Louis Ford	
1915–1919	Harry Linney	
1919–1926	Peter Hodge	Second Division Champions 1924/1925
1926–1934	William Orr	First Division Runners-up 1928/29 (highest League finish)
1932–1934	Peter Hodge	
1934–1936	Arthur Lochhead	
1936–1939	Frank Womack	Second Division Champions 1936/37
1939–1945	Tom Bromilow	
1945/1946	Tom Mather	
1946–1949	Johnny Duncan	FA Cup Runners-up 1949
1949–1955	Norman Bullock	Second Division Champions 1953/54
1955–1958	David Halliday	Second Division Champions 1956/57

1958–1968	Matt Gillies	FA Cup Runners-up 1961 & '63 League Cup Winners 1964 Runners-up 1965
1968–1971	Frank O'Farrell	FA Cup Runners-up 1969 Second Division Champions 1970/1971
1971–1977	Jimmy Bloomfield	
1977/1978	Frank McLintock	
1978–1982	Jock Wallace	Second Division Champions 1979/80
1982–1986	Gordon Milne	Promoted to the First Division 1982/83
1986/1987	Gordon Milne and Bryan Hamilton	
1987	Bryan Hamilton	
1987–1991	David Pleat	
1991–1994	Brian Little	Promoted to the Premier League 1993/94
1994/1995	Mark McGhee	
1995–2000	Martin O'Neill	Promoted to the Premier League 1995/96 League Cup winner '97 & 2000 Runners-up 1999
2000–2001	Peter Taylor	
2001/2002	Dave Bassett	
2002–2004	Micky Adams	First Division Runners-up 2002/03
2004–2006	Craig Levein	
2006/2007	Rob Kelly	
2007	Martin Allen	
2007	Gary Megson	
2007/2008	Ian Holloway	
2008–2010	Nigel Pearson	League One Champions 2008/09

2010   Paulo Sousa
2010/2011   Sven-Göran Eriksson
2011–Present   Nigel Pearson   Championship Champions
                                     2013/14

MAN CITY CONNECTION

A number of former Manchester City managers and/or players have managed the Foxes – and vice versa. The most notable of all is Roberto Mancini, who arrived on loan at Filbert Street in 2001 and stayed for five games before being tempted back to Italy, where he took his first steps into management. Mancini would later manage Man City from 2009 to 2013, winning the Premier League in 2012. Sven-Göran Eriksson managed Manchester City between 2007 and 2008 before eventually arriving at the Walkers Stadium in 2010, where, of course, he took on Mancini in the FA Cup, a game won by the Sky Blues after a replay. Martin O'Neill briefly played for Manchester City in 1981/82, making thirteen appearances before moving on, and Gary Megson was at Maine Road between 1989 and 1992 and managed the Foxes briefly in 2007. Finally, Peter Hodge sandwiched six years with Manchester City in between his two spells with the Foxes.

JUST LIKE WATCHING BRAZIL

The King Power Stadium can rightly claim to have hosted the biggest names in world football over the past few years, with England, Brazil and Real Madrid all playing at the Foxes' home in recent years. Let's start with international matches. A year after the stadium opened, England played an international friendly against Serbia and Montenegro – when the two countries played as one – and the people of Leicester turned out in force. Steven Gerrard scored the first-ever England goal at what was then the Walkers Stadium but Serbia and Montenegro equalised on half-time through Jestrovic. Joe Cole scored what proved to be the winning goal on 82 minutes as England secured a 2-1 win in front of 30,900 fans.

3 June 2003
England   2–1   Serbia and Montenegro
Gerrard 35   Jestrovic 45
J. Cole 82

Attendance: 30,900

The second international played at Leicester just four months later was again a crowd puller with Jamaica taking on Brazil. A capacity 32,000 saw Roberto Carlos score the only goal of the game on 15 minutes.

12 October 2003
Jamaica   0-1   Brazil
                R. Carlos 15

Attendance: 32,000

It would be three years before another international game was played at City's home was Jamaica *v*. Ghana, with future manager Appiah scoring twice for the Africans in a 4-1 win.

Jamaica   1-4   Ghana
Euell 58   Muntari 5
                Stewart 19 (o.g)
                Appiah 66, 68

Attendance: Unconfirmed

THE REAL DEAL

Perhaps the Foxes' highest profile friendly ever was in the preseason of 2011/12, when La Liga giants Real Madrid arrived in the East Midlands as part of the preparations for the new campaign. The match attracted a record attendance (football) of 32,188.

Leicester City	1-2	Real Madrid
Dyer 88		Callejon 43
		Benzema 61

Attendance: 32,188

The teams for this historic fixture were:

Leicester City: Schmeichel, Peltier, Mills (St. Ledger 44), Bamba, Konchesky (Ball 75), Vassell (Dyer 75), Danns (Waghorn 75), Abe (Oakley 75), Wellens (Johnson half-time), Gallagher (King 46), Nugent (Howard 75). Subs: Berner, Weale, Schlupp, Tunchev

Real Madrid: Adan (Casillas half-time), Ramos, Albiol (Fernandez 80), Varane, Marcelo (Arbeloa 63), Coentrao, Khedira (Pepe 63), Granero (Ozil half-time), Callejon (Ronaldo 46), Kaka (Alonso half-time), Benzema (Higuain 63). Subs: Carvalho, Sahin, Mejias, Casado, Rodriguez

CLUB HONOURS – IN BRIEF

Domestic competitions

League
English first tier (currently Premier League)
Runners-up: 1928/29
English second tier (currently Football League Championship)

Champions: 1924/25, 1936/37, 1953/54, 1956/57, 1970/71, 1979/80, 2013/14
Runners-up: 1907/08, 2002/03
Play-off winners: 1993/94, 1995/96
Pay-off runners-up: 1991/92, 1992/93
English third tier (currently Football League One)
Champions: 2008/09

Cup Competitions
FA Cup Runners-up: 1949, 1961, 1963, 1969
Football League Cup Winners: 1964, 1997, 2000
Runners-up: 1965, 1999
FA Charity Shield Winners: 1971
Regional Competitions
War League South Champions: 1942
Midland War Cup Winners: 1941

LEAGUE OF OUR OWN

Since election to the football league in 1894, the Foxes have spent a number of years bouncing between the divisions, mostly in the top two tiers of English football. City have played outside the top two tiers only once – during the 2008/09 season City played in League One, the third tier of English football, but were promoted back as champion after just one season and the Foxes have never played in the fourth tier of English football.

The record in chronological order:

1894–1908	Division Two
1908–1909	Division One
1909–1925	Division Two
1925–1935	Division One

1935–1937	Division Two
1937–1939	Division One
1946–1954	Division Two
1954–1955	Division One
1955–1957	Division Two
1957–1969	Division One
1969–1971	Division Two
1971–1978	Division One
1978–1980	Division Two
1980–1981	Division One
1981–1983	Division Two
1983–1987	Division One
1987–1992	Division Two
1992–1994	Division One
1994–1995	Premier League
1995–1996	Division One
1996–2002	Premier League
2002–2003	Division One
2003–2004	Premier League
2004–2008	Championship
2008–2009	League One
2009–2014	Championship
2014–Present	Premier League

SIX SWANS LEGEND

Did a flock of swans really have magical powers or was it pure coincidence? The people inside Filbert Street on 20 October 1928 will tell you something odd happened when City took on Portsmouth, with the Foxes on the verge of creating a little piece of history. City were 7-0 up, Arthur Chandler having scored five of the goals. Ernie Hine grabbed number eight as five swans flew over Filbert Street, matching Chandler's incredible feat the supporters took it as a sign and when a straggling sixth swan flew over the stadium, the fans took that as a message from the heavens that Chandler was destined to complete a double hat-trick. With the fans urging him on, he did exactly that, matching the number of swans who had unknowingly become part of Leicester City folklore. City went on to win 10-0 and record the club's biggest-ever win.

1969 FA CUP FINAL

While the Foxes would be playing their third FA Cup final of the decade, Manchester City had been waiting since Bert Trautmann won the hearts of a nation as well as the Cup for the Sky Blues when he played the last 20 minutes of the 1956 occasion with a broken neck.

Manchester City came into the 1968/69 season as defending champions, but so abject had their title defence been, it seemed the players (virtually the same XI that had won the League with such swagger) decided the FA Cup represented a very acceptable consolation prize.

For the Foxes, it was a chance to at last end the losing final sequence that was becoming a psychological barrier in the minds of the players.

The Cup run had brought the very best out of Joe Mercer's side and this was their shot at redemption – proof that the best team in the land had actually just lost their way somewhere in the bread and butter of League football.

The teams had already met twice in the League that season. The Foxes had defeated the Sky Blues 3-0 at Filbert Street, and Manchester City had won the return game 2-0 courtesy of a Mike Summerbee brace.

The Foxes had edged past Barnsley in the third round, drawing 1-1 at Oakwell before finishing the job 2-1 at Filbert

Street. They then did just enough to see off Millwall in round four with a 1-0 win at The Den.

With the threat of relegation all too real for Leicester, the team seemed to be free of the shackles of their League form in the Cup. However, when Liverpool left Filbert Street with a 0-0 draw in the fifth round, it looked likely the adventure would end in disappointment, but just two days later, with Peter Shilton at his brilliant best keeping everything the Reds could throw at him out, Tommy Smith's penalty meant that Andy Lochhead's goal was the classic smash-and-grab winner to leave almost 55,000 Anfield fans stunned. Yet another narrow win over lower League opposition – this time a 1-0 win over Mansfield Town at Field Mill – and the Foxes, second bottom in Division One were now in the semi-final. Could this finally be our year? A 1-0 win over West Brom at Hillsborough suggested it just might and as City lined up for their fifth cup final of the decade, hopes were high among the fans from East Midlands that their time had come.

Sky Blues coach Malcolm Allison told his players to hang back for a minute or two to deliberately keep the Leicester players waiting in the tunnel. It was a proud moment for both Joe Mercer and Leicester boss Frank O'Farrell as they led their teams out for the jewel in the crown of English football's domestic season.

For Leicester in particular, staring relegation in the face having already lost thirteen away games that season, reaching Wembley yet again was a minor miracle. Manchester City started well but the Foxes, revelling in their role as underdogs, grew in confidence and created a number of chances as the match ebbed and flowed.

Both Clarke and Rodrigues had opportunities to give the East Midlands outfit the lead. Clarke saw his shot brilliantly saved by Harry Dowd, and Rodrigues somehow missed a cross from a couple of yards out as he sliced the ball wide from close range. Just 3 minutes after that miss, the Foxes paid a heavy price – Neil Young finally broke the deadlock as he rifled an unstoppable shot past Shilton and into the roof of the net to give his team a 1-0 lead.

Dowd preserved Manchester City's slender advantage with several fine saves after the break and was the Sky Blues' outstanding performer on the day – the fact that he was the Man of the Match proves the Foxes were more than a tad unfortunate on the day, but despite their best efforts, Mercer's side hung on to claim a memorable victory and ensure the FA Cup final jinx continued for Leicester. The stats for the final are:

FA Cup final
26 April 1969
Manchester City   1-0   Leicester City

Man City: Dowd, Book, Pardoe, Doyle, Booth, Oakes, Summerbee, Bell, Lee, Coleman, Young.
Manager: Joe Mercer
Leicester City: Shilton, Rodrigues, Nish, Roberts, Woollett, Cross, Fern, Gibson, Lochhead, Clarke, Glover (Manley 70).
Manager: Frank O'Farrell
Referee: George McCabe
Wembley Stadium
Attendance: 100,000

FRANK WORTHINGTON: CITY CULT HERO

Here is small section on a player who is still talked about in revered tones by City fans – Frank Worthington. Some quotes, facts and a fans' profile:

Name: Frank Worthington
Years: 1972–1977
Position: Forward
Date of Birth: Tuesday 23 November 1948
Place of birth: Halifax
City debut: Wednesday 23 August 1972, scoring in a 1-1 draw at Manchester United
Appearances: 209 + 1 as a substitute
Goals: 72

Season breakdown (League only)

Season	Played	Scored
1973/1974	42	20 goals (Division One)
1974/1975	42	18 goals (Division One)
1975/1976	39	9 goals (Division One)
1976/1977	41	14 goals (Division One)
1977/1978	7	1 goal (Division One)

Frankie said:

• 'Elvis is the King!! I'm the world's biggest fan. A mate of mine, Peter Rudge, got me an Elvis neck chain off the main man's Dad, Vernon. On it is inscribed T.C.B, which is on Elvis's grave. It stands for "Taking Care of Business".'

• 'My best goal? Remember my goal for Bolton against Ipswich. I turned to Terry Butcher afterwards and told him "if he had been standing on the terracing with the supporters, he might have had a better view of it".'

• 'I was lucky to play with some quality players. Tony Evans at Birmingham was tremendous, a great lad and a great finisher. I played with Kevin Keegan for England and we struck up a good partnership. So much so, that Bill Shankly tried to sign me for Liverpool, but I failed my medical due to high blood pressure.'

An Ode to Frank Worthington
By Richard Stanley and Gary Silke from *The Fox,* 1990

A young Yorkshireman called Frank Worthington first came to the attention of Foxes fans in the 1969/70 season when City were away at Huddersfield. I was listening to the radio and the commentator was in raptures about the home side's centre forward. In those days Huddersfield were quite a successful team and even enjoyed a spell in the First Division. However they were still obliged to sell a talent as big as Worthington and he came to Leicester in August 1972.

He already had a reputation as something of a showman, turning up for an England under-23 tour in a sombrero, amazing the locals of some far off nation.

So we at Filbert Street found that we had a great footballer and an entertainer as well. During the pre-match kick-in he would exhibit his excellent ball control by keeping the ball up for a minute or two with either foot, then he would flick it over his head, catch it on the back of his neck, hold it there for a moment, then gradually stand up straight, rolling the ball down his spine, back-heeling it back over his head to continue with his feet. The kids on the wall at the front of the Kop would stand agog, and many an hour must have been spent in the backyards of Leicester trying, just once, to emulate this trick. Everything about the man was flash – even when the Kopites sang his name he responded with an enthusiastic double hand wave and while waiting for corners he would often use the time to assemble his hair.

A performance of Wortho's forever etched in my mind occurred in the winter of '72 when West Brom came down to Filbert Street. He scored a hat-trick and centre-backs John Wile and Ally Robertson were as good as any at that time. But Worthington was far too good for them and if he had been 'Big Daddy' he would have been banging their heads together. That was Worthington 'on his day' – The Best. Other times he could appear disinterested, but he was never less than entertaining.

Frank soon played for England under caretaker manager of Joe Mercer. He looked perfectly at home in the white shirt and scored against Argentina with an incredible bicycle kick, which *Shoot!* magazine felt compelled to break down into a series of four photos under the title 'Frank's Cowboy Kick'. Unfortunately, the Don Revie era was just about to happen and there would be no room for someone with as much flair as Wortho. Workmanlike ethics and dossiers (and failure) became the mid-seventies way, and Wortho's international career was over before it had begun. Which was a shame for England as well as the man himself because with a little more experience and pace at top level we could have had something approaching another Johan Cruyff. His skill could be compared to anyone.

In the disastrous season of '77/78 relegation was nothing compared to the departure of Wortho. He left a big gap at Filbert Street which has not been properly filled since. He went back up North to Bolton Wanderers and took to wearing a red headband to add a little panache, as if it were needed. At Bolton he scored 'that goal' which will be shown on football programmes until the end of time.

After that he took up a nomadic existence throughout the eighties popping up at a dozen different clubs and Leicester fans, especially, would always like to know where he was, keeping tabs on him ready for the next time that someone would ask 'Where's Wortho these days?'

Prior to joining City Frank was all set to sign for Bill Shankly at Liverpool but failed the medical. Fact, or fiction, has it that in the summer prior to this he had been on holiday with George Best. Hand on heart it has to be said that playing for Liverpool may have been his rightful stage. However, to his credit Wortho did not outwardly dwell on this point and I feel he enjoyed his time at Leicester. Frank, wherever you are, thanks for the glorious memories and wonderful entertainment...

WHAT'S ALL THE FOSSE ABOUT? A BRIEF HISTORY OF LEICESTER FOSSE...

The club we know and love as Leicester City began life as Leicester Fosse in 1894 due to the fact the decision to form the club was taken in a shack off Fosse Road. In truly romantic fashion, the players donated a small sum of money in the form of a subscription and a local carpenter was entrusted with making two sets of goal posts in preparation of the fledgling club's first fixture on a field close to Fosse Road. The first match was against Syston Fosse and, with the players wearing black shirts with a blue sash and white shorts, ended in a 5-0 win for Leicester, the historic first scorers being Hilton Johnson (2), Arthur West (2) and Sam Dingley.

Quite rightly, the History Boys are listed here – the first Fosse team ever: Smith, Burdett, E. Johnson, W. Johnson, Garner, H. Johnson, Lewitt, West, Bromwich, Ashby, Dingley. The irony surely can't be lost on any Midlander that Fosse had both a 'West' and a 'Bromwich' in the starting XI!

Fosse played several more games that season at Victoria Park. It wasn't until 1887 that the club moved to slightly better surrounds at the Belgrave Road Sports Ground, but after being outbid for the right to continue renting the facilities at their new home, Fosse's stay lasted just twelve months before a return to Victoria Park was the only logical alternative. If the club was to really kick on, it needed to find a better home pitch – and quickly. Fortunately, a new venue was identified at Mill Lane – owned by the council and situated by a canal. Fosse were accepted as members of the Football Association in 1890, and for the new season the colours were changed to white shirts and blue shorts. Being a member of the FA brought with it entry into the prestigious English Cup, but the first experience Fosse had was a 4-0 Mill Lane defeat to Burton Wanderers.

Things were looking up and in December 1890, a local derby

with rivals Loughborough saw 2,500 fans pay record receipts. The season ended on a high with a friendly against League opposition for the first time in the shape of Notts County, who had reached, but lost, the final of the English Cup that season. A 2-2 draw in front of another record crowd suggested Fosse were ready to take the next step up, and in 1891 application was made, and accepted, to The Midland League. As was the way of the day, building work was to be undertaken on the Mill Lane plot of land and was no longer a viable option for the club. Fosse moved on again, this time to Aylestone Cricket Ground where they would also suffer a first qualifying FA Cup defeat at the hands of Small Heath, who left the East Midlands with a 6-2 victory.

In 1892, Fosse moved again (perhaps Leicester Wanderers would have been more apt), hanging their collective hats at the Walnut Street Ground, where Fosse no doubt hoped to prove difficult to crack. As the ground was steadily improved, towards the end of the 1892/93 campaign, a clash with Loughborough drew in 13,000 paying spectators. A year later, however, when Bootle resigned from the Football League's Second Division, Fosse were invited to take their place. Graciously, Fosse declined the offer, feeling a sense of duty to give the Midland League more notice. In 1894, Fosse felt it was time to up the ante and applied successfully for election to the Football League Second Division. The club had paid their dues, grown beyond recognition and were now ready to mix it with the big boys.

Fosse's first League fixture was a 4-3 defeat away to Grimsby Town with the first victory a 4-2 win over Rotherham Town at Walnut Street, which would eventually be renamed Filbert Street. Fosse would continue to exist until 1919 – and be reborn as Leicester City when the League resumed after the First World War.

SO CLOSE...

City came within just a point of being crowned English champions in 1928/29 – the closest the club has come to the ultimate domestic prize in their 130-year history. With the greatest City strike force of all-time leading the line in the form of Arthur Chandler, Arthur Lochead and Ernie Hine, the battle for the title would go to the very last few weeks of the campaign. With two games remaining, City were still three points behind but with a better goal average, but a draw with Huddersfield Town and a similar result for Sheffield Wednesday (known as The Wednesday back then) left the Foxes three points adrift with just one game remaining. The goals of the holy trinity had propelled City steadily up the table after a disappointing start to the season that saw just two wins out of the first eight games, resulting in a fourteenth-place spot in the table. There were good runs along the way – one such burst of form saw Portsmouth thrashed 10-0 at Filbert Street – and City climbed up to second spot with five games to go. City played their game in hand against relegation-threatened Portsmouth, knowing a win would put them just two points behind The Wednesday. But Pompey, still licking their wounds from the ten-goal mauling by the Foxes earlier in the campaign, were perhaps the worst team City could have faced. The Fratton Park side were driven focused, determined and belied their lowly position by winning 1-0. Revenge was sweet and hopes began to fade that the title would be heading back to Filbert Street. City finished second, and the fact that half of the club's games that season had failed to end in victory (and the Foxes still only missed out by one point) suggests that there was never a better time to win the League. Ah, well...

First Division final table, 1928/29:

Position		P	W	D	L	F	A	Pts
1	The Wednesday	42	21	10	11	86	62	52
2	Leicester City	42	21	9	12	96	67	51
3	Aston Villa	42	23	4	15	98	81	50
4	Sunderland	42	20	7	15	93	75	47
5	Liverpool	42	17	12	13	90	64	46
6	Derby County	42	18	10	14	86	71	46
7	Blackburn Rovers	42	17	11	14	72	63	45
8	Manchester City	42	18	9	15	95	86	45
9	Arsenal	42	16	13	13	77	72	45
10	Newcastle United	42	19	6	17	70	72	44
11	Sheffield United	42	15	11	16	86	85	41
12	Manchester United	42	14	13	15	66	76	41
13	Leeds United	42	16	9	17	71	84	41
14	Bolton Wanderers	42	14	12	16	73	80	40
15	Birmingham	42	15	10	17	68	77	40
16	Huddersfield Town	42	14	11	17	70	61	39
17	West Ham United	42	15	9	18	86	96	39
18	Everton	42	17	4	21	63	75	38
19	Burnley	42	15	8	19	81	103	38
20	Portsmouth	42	15	6	21	56	80	36
21	Bury	42	12	7	23	62	99	31
22	Cardiff City	42	8	13	21	43	59	29

JINX TEAMS (LEAGUE ONLY)

Every team has bogey teams – clubs that, historically, you just don't seem to well against. City are no exception, and there are several clubs who have inexplicably good records against the Foxes. We're not talking about Manchester United, Chelsea, Arsenal or Liverpool – everyone has a bad record against them!

City's jinx teams are, with respect, anything but high flyers. Let's being...

Fulham

In seventy-two meetings with the Cottagers, City have failed to win fifty-two times – that's pretty poor. Fulham are traditionally poor travellers, yet they've enjoyed fifteen victories in Leicester and left with five draws secured – the Foxes have managed just sixteen wins on their own soil in this fixture. At Craven Cottage, it's even worse, with City failing to win on thirty-one of their thirty-six trips to Craven Cottage. Overall, it adds up to a dismal return. The last time the Foxes beat Fulham home and away in the same season was in the 1982/83 campaign.

Preston North End

Just twelve of fifty-two League meetings between City and Preston North End have ended with a Foxes victory. The Lilywhites have won twenty-five and drawn fifteen of the clashes and between 1970 and 2010, and North End won five of their eight trips to Filbert Street and The Walkers Stadium, drawing two and losing just once before a 1-0 defeat in October 2010.

Huddersfield Town

Another surprise jinx team, Huddersfield have generally enjoyed playing the Foxes over the years – though this has improved in recent times, with the Foxes winning the last seven meetings home and away. Prior to this, the Foxes and had well and truly had their tails bitten by the Terriers, who had won twenty-seven and drawn eight of the fifty-one meetings between the two clubs. Huddersfield's record in Leicester is impressive having won twelve of their twenty-eight meetings, drawing three games and losing only thirteen.

Southampton

Southampton's jinx is confined to the south coast, with City's 2-0 win at St Mary's in 2012 only City's third win in thirty-five visits! The Foxes failed to win any of the games played at The Dell between 1922 and 1967 before finally winning 5-1 and ending a 13-match winless run. Spurs have won more times away to City than they have at White Hart Lane! Spurs have won twenty-two of their forty-four League meetings at Filbert Street (a 50 per cent win ratio), drawing six and losing sixteen. Spurs have only managed 19 wins at White Hart Lane, with City enjoying fourteen wins and eleven draws, making it one of our luckiest grounds.

NAVY BLUES

England's two major naval dockyard teams, Plymouth Argyle and Portsmouth, both share something in common: an appalling record away to Leicester City. In fact, two of the Foxes' best percentage records of victory are against Pompey and the Pilgrims. Portsmouth once suffered a 10-0 defeat at Filbert Street, but that's just the tip of the iceberg. In twenty-six league visits to the East Midlands, Pompey have managed just two wins since 1935, meaning they've returned to the south coast on twenty-four occasions having lost or drawn. Plymouth's record isn't much better – in fact, it's worse. In nineteen trips to Leicester, they've won just once, drawn four and lost fourteen times. Both sides have much better records on their own grounds, it has to be said, but it's also fair to say that both consider the Foxes to be a bogey side on the road. It would be churlish not to mention the side City enjoy playing at home to most – Doncaster Rovers, who have lost fourteen of their visits to the Foxes home ground, drawing one and winning the other. In fact, it has been 112 years since Doncaster won in Leicester!

BRUM, BRUM!

City have played Birmingham City more times than any other club. With the fixture stretching back to 1896/97, the teams have been in the same division on sixty-two occasions over the past 118 years, with 124 meetings in total. For the record, the Foxes have won fifty-one times, Blues have won fifty and there have been twenty-three draws. You can add nine more meetings between the teams in the Cup to total 133 clashes, but City have never lost a match in a knock-out competition to their Midlands cousins, winning six and drawing three. Arsenal are City's next most-played sides, with no less than 131 meetings in League – the Gunners having won sixty of those, while another London side, West Ham, account for 121 meetings to date. The Hammers have the upper hand in the League meetings, having fifty times, drawn twenty-nine and lost thirty-eight. Leeds United are next with 120 meetings in all competitions.

APRIL FOOLS?

City haven't won a fixture played on April Fool's Day since 1992 – some six matches ago. The Foxes have won eight of the twenty-five games played, lost eight and drawn the other eleven.

LOSS OFF THE PITCH

Leicester Fosse thought they'd done a nifty piece of business by bringing in experienced centre-half Ted Pheasant from Wolverhampton Wanderers in time for the 1910/11 campaign. The thirty-three-year-old was the ideal addition for the Foxes, but within two weeks, Ted had died of peritonitis at Leicester Infirmary.

GIBBO!

No less than five Leicester City stars have had the surname Gibson. Dr Thomas Gibson was the first to play for the club in 1926, though he only made four appearances before moving to new pastures. George Gibson was next up in 1934, but he also made only a handful of appearances – just two – before moving on. David Gibson arrived in 1962, and is easily the longest-serving of the Gibsons, making 333 appearances between 1962 and 1970. William Gibson spent three years at Filbert Street from 1979 to 1982, and the last of the clan, Colin, who stayed with City for four years between 1990 and 1994, made seventy-four appearances in all competitions.

PERFECT MATCH

Three former City strikers have gone on to enjoy excellent careers in the media, and are regularly on Saturday night television. Gary Lineker has presented *Match of the Day* for more than a decade, and Steve Claridge follows Gary's show as part of a two-man presenting team on *The Football League Show*. Robbie Savage is a regular guest on *Football Focus* and BBC Radio 5 Live's 606 Show, and Les Ferdinand has enjoyed an on-off career in the media, appearing on *Match of the Day* and other football programmes since his retirement from the game. Stan Collymore has one of the radio's most popular phone-ins on TalkSport, so it clearly pays to have been a Fox!

WAR GAMES

The Foxes, like every other club in Britain, were forced to play in regional divisions during the First and Second World Wars. From 1915 to 1919, Leicester Fosse entered the Midland League, whereas Leicester City went into the Midland, South, National and North leagues from 1939 to 1946. The best City managed was to top the South League, a division of thirteen clubs including Norwich City, West Brom, Wolves, Luton Town and Nottingham Forest. The gates rarely topped 4,000, but almost 8,000 turned out for the City *v.* Forest game, proving that despite the ongoing conflicts, the interest in the derby match was still strong.

AWAY WOE

City's worst-ever away run began on 18 October 1986 with a 2-0 defeat at Charlton Athletic, which was followed by a 4-1 thrashing at Liverpool in the Littlewoods Cup. A 2-0 loss at Villa Park made it three in a row, but things were about to get worse with a 5-1 defeat at Watford. The Foxes put up a better display in the M69 derby against Coventry, where only a Cyril Regis strike separated the sides at Highfield Road. However, trips to Goodison Park to face Manchester United and Everton ended in 2-0 and 5-1 defeats respectively, as Gordon Milne and Bryan Hamilton's side slipped to the foot of the table and were now in serious relegation trouble. There was to be little joy at jink ground Upton Park where the Hammers triumphed 4-1 at the start of the New Year. Despite beating Sheffield Wednesday 6-1 at Filbert Street, the Foxes still couldn't cure their travel sickness after a 5-2 defeat to QPR at Loftus Road in the FA Cup third round. The 1-0 defeat at Luton Town made it ten losses in a row away from home. Despite a spirited effort at

Anfield, Liverpool still took all three points after edging a seven-goal thriller, and Spurs rounded off February with a 2-0 reverse at White Hart Lane. With a dozen straight defeats, the annual defeat at The Dell followed by a 4-0 thrashing from Southampton – courtesy mainly of a Matt Le Tissier hat-trick. Nottingham Forest rubbed salt in the wounds with a crushing 2-1 derby defeat at the City Ground, and Newcastle United made it fifteen straight losses with a 2-0 win at St James' Park. The dismal run was never going to end at Highbury. The graveyard of many better City sides than that of 1986/87, and the 4-1 drubbing was the expected outcome in North London. So with sixteen beatings in a row, City went to Chelsea in search of a the win that could still help them avoid relegation, but a 3-1 loss at Stamford Bridge made escape unlikely, especially after Charlton Athletic's three points put the Foxes back into the bottom three with two games remaining. A home draw with Coventry left City needing to better Charlton's result to move ahead of the Addicks on the final day, but despite bringing the dreadful sequence to an end with a 0-0 draw at the Manor Ground against Oxford, Charlton's win meant relegation for the Foxes. The first three games of the Division Two campaign all ended in defeat before, finally, a 3-2 win at Bournemouth got City back on track, but a new club record of seventeen successive losses had already been posted and a dreadful run of twenty-one games without success was at an end.

GERMAN LESSONS

City embarked on a highly successful tour of Germany as part of the 1966/67 preseason build-up. The Foxes began with a superb 3-0 win over Borussia Mönchengladbach courtesy of goals from Stringfellow, Roberts and Sinclair. Then, Bundesliga 2 outfit RSV Gottingen 05 were comfortably beaten 4-1 with the goals scored by Stringfellow (2) and Sinclair (2). The tour was completed with a 3-1 win over Werder Bremen, Stringfellow and Sinclair again on target and Dougan also finding the net. The tour was deemed so successful that the Fox returned to Germany a year later, though FC Kaiserslautern ensured things got off to a tougher start with a 1-0 defeat for City. Eintracht Braunschweig were next up, and goals from Nish and Roberts secured a 2-1 victory. The games seemed tougher with the opposition perhaps a notch up from the previous year. VfB Stuttgart proved another tough nut to crack, but ultimately a Sinclair penalty was enough to see off the Germans.

NIL BY HABIT

If title-winning sides really are built on solid foundations, the Foxes side of 1921/22 should have been destined for great things. Having kept seventeen clean sheets the previous campaign, Peter Hodge's mean machine kept no less than twenty clean sheets during the 1921/2 season, with a further two shut-outs in the FA Cup. Unfortunately, that didn't necessarily equate to exciting football or silverware as Fosse failed to score on sixteen occasions in the League. There were also nine 0-0 draws and Jock Paterson's total of seven goals was enough to top the scoring charts!

YULETIDE CHEER

Johnny Duncan's Christmas came right on cue when he bagged six goals against Port Vale on Christmas Day 1924. The Foxes won 7-0 as Duncan forged a prolific partnership with Arthur Chandler during the 1924/25 campaign as City romped to the

Division Two title and the pair bagged a combined sixty-two goals between them.

IZZET MUZZY?

City's all-time Premier League goalscorer from 1992 to 2014 is none less than London-born Muzzy Izzet. Muzzy was signed by Martin O'Neill initially on loan from Chelsea in March 1996, before a permanent deal of £800,000 was agreed. After playing a vital role in promotion back to the top flight, he scored his first Premier League goal away to Aston Villa. His last was during a 3-2 defeat to Leeds United before moving to Birmingham City after eight years' sterling service. He managed thirty-three top-flight goals in total and he fell just one shy of fifty goals for City in total.

JELLY ON A PLATE

One of City's best named players from the past is undoubtedly Ted Jelly, who stayed at Filbert Street from 1946 to 1951. Jelly was a former sailor and played for the Foxes sixty-five times before moving on to Plymouth Argyle. A right-winger by trade, his record of one goal during his five-year stay suggests he was prone to the odd wobble in the box.

CENTURIONS

City's best goalscoring season was during the 1956/57 campaign, when Foxes players found the net 109 times on their way to promotion from Division Two. It was a particularly prolific season for striker Arthur Rowley, who played in all forty-two League games and netted an incredible forty-four goals, including four hat-tricks. There were some real goal fests with City scoring four goals twice, five goals on six occasions, six goals on two occasions and seven in one match. The defence wasn't exactly watertight with only seven clean sheets all season, but it mattered little as the Foxes were crowned champions having topped the table almost exclusively from October onwards.

ROCK AND A SUNNY PLACE

City embarked on postseason break in the sunshine in May 1962, heading for a two-match tour of Gibraltar and Spain in the process. Gibraltar were comfortably dispatched 5-0 thanks to goals from Walsh, Riley, Keyworth (2) and McLintock. Keyworth was again on target four days later, scoring the only goal in a 1-0 win over Malaga.

SPOT OF BOTHER?

It's a fair bet that City's leading penalty kick scorer will never be caught, given the nature of today's shorter-serving players. Arthur Rowley notched up an incredible forty-one successful penalties – thirty-eight coming in the League and a further three in the FA Cup during an eight-year stay at Filbert Street between 1950 and 1958. Rowley actually missed another eight! Some way behind is Sep Smith, with twenty-six successful spot kicks and Steve Lynex is third with twenty-three. Completing the top five are Gary McAllister with fifteen in total and tied in fifth are David Nish and Bob Pollock with fourteen each. It's worth noting that the club's all-time record goalscorer Arthur Chandler tried to convert a penalty on two occasions, missing each time!

The 1985/86 season saw an unusually high number of penalties awarded to the Foxes – fifteen being awarded during the campaign. While eleven were converted, four were missed. Lynex notched seven of them, McAllister scored two and Ian Banks bagged one. Only in 1933/34 were no penalties awarded either for or against City – the only occasion that has happened. In 2006/07, the Foxes gave away thirteen penalties, only one of which was saved. Lynex proved what a sportsman he was in September 1982 when City were playing Carlisle United. Three penalties were awarded, and with Lynex already having two in the bag, he had the chance to create a unique piece of history by bagging a third penalty against the hapless Cumbrians. Lynex – who had already completed his hat-trick – gave the kick to promising young striker Gary Lineker, who duly converted the penalty to complete a 6-0 victory. The quickest penalty conceded was away to Liverpool when the Foxes found themselves up against it after just 19 seconds. Alec Lindsay converted the kick and later scored another to render Keith Weller's strike meaningless on the day. For the record, only three players have scored penalties for and against the Foxes during their career – Paul Dickov, Mike Newell and Reg Halton.

PAYING CUSTOMERS

There have been various records set by Foxes fans at Filbert Street and the Walkers Stadium/the King Power Stadium over the years in various competitions. Here are the games when City's ground was fit to bursting.

Highest home attendance
The highest City crowd of all-time was 47,298 *v.* Tottenham Hotspur at Filbert Street, during an FA Cup fifth round on 18

February 1928 at a time when the competition was breaking club records up and down the country.

Highest home league attendance
Spurs' North London rivals Arsenal were the side City set a new League attendance record against when 42,486 crammed into Filbert Street for the First Division clash on 2 October 1954.

Highest home attendance in the second tier (Championship and predecessors)
On 17 November 1956, a massive gate of 40,830 came to watch the East Midlands clash with Nottingham Forest at Filbert Street.

Highest home attendance in the third tier (League One and predecessors)
As the Foxes edged towards promotion in 2009, a crowd of 30,542 packed the Walkers Stadium to watch City take on Scunthorpe United on 24 April 2009.

Highest home FA Cup attendance
Again, the 47,298 *v.* Tottenham Hotspur in February 1928 – see record crowd at the top of this list.

Highest home League Cup attendance
It's been a while since the League Cup was a real crowd puller, but the 35,121 that attended the fifth round tie against West Bromwich Albion at Filbert Street on 29 October 1969 was proof that there was a thirst for the competition during its first decade of existence.

Highest average attendance for a League season
The best average gate in City's history was set during the

1957/58 campaign, when the Foxes posted an average crowd of 31,359 in the First Division.

Highest attendance at the Walkers Stadium
Since leaving Filbert Street in 2001, the highest crowd recorded at the Foxes' new home is 32,148, when Newcastle United were the visitors for a Premier League clash on Boxing Day 2003.

STATS SECTION

Leicester City's complete league history

Season	League	Position
2014/15	Barclays Premier League	8th/20
2013/14	Skybet Championship	1st/24
2012/13	npower Championship	6th/24
2011/12	npower Championship	9th/24
2010/11	npower Championship	10th/24
2009/10	Coca-Cola Championship	5th/24
2008/09	Coca-Cola League One	1st/24
2007/08	Coca-Cola Championship	22nd/24
2006/07	Coca-Cola Championship	19th/24
2005/06	Coca Cola Championship	16th/24
2004/05	Coca-Cola Championship	15th/24
2003/04	Barclaycard Premiership	18th/20
2002/03	Nationwide League Division One	2nd/24
2001/02	FA Barclaycard Premiership	20th/20
2000/01	FA Carling Premiership	13th/20
1999/00	FA Carling Premiership	8th/20
1998/99	FA Carling Premiership	10th/20
1997/98	FA Carling Premiership	10th/20
1996/97	FA Carling Premiership	9th/20
1995/96	Endsleigh League Division One	5th*/24
1994/95	FA Carling Premiership	21st/22
1993/94	Endsleigh League Division One	4th*/24
1992/93	Barclays League Division One	6th/24
1991/92	Barclays Second Division	4th/24
1990/91	Barclays Second Division	22nd/24

	Home					Away					
Pld	W	D	L	F	A	W	D	L	F	A	Pts
0	0	0	0	0	0	0	0	0	0	0	0
46	17	4	2	46	22	14	5	4	37	21	102
46	13	4	6	46	23	6	7	10	25	25	68
46	11	6	6	36	22	7	6	10	30	33	66
46	13	6	4	48	27	6	4	13	28	44	67
46	13	6	4	40	18	8	7	8	21	27	76
46	13	9	1	41	16	14	6	3	43	23	96
46	7	7	9	23	19	5	9	9	19	26	52
46	6	8	9	26	31	7	6	10	23	33	53
46	8	9	6	30	25	5	6	12	21	34	54
46	8	8	7	24	20	4	13	6	25	26	57
38	3	10	6	19	28	3	5	11	29	37	33
46	16	5	2	40	12	10	9	4	33	28	92
38	3	7	9	15	34	2	6	11	15	30	28
38	10	4	5	28	23	4	2	13	11	28	48
38	10	3	6	31	24	6	4	9	24	31	55
38	7	6	6	25	25	5	7	7	15	21	49
38	6	10	3	21	15	7	4	8	30	26	53
38	7	5	7	22	26	5	6	8	24	28	47
46	9	7	7	32	29	10	7	6	34	31	71
42	5	6	10	28	37	1	5	15	17	43	29
46	11	9	3	45	30	8	7	8	27	29	73
46	14	5	4	43	24	8	5	10	28	40	76
46	14	4	5	41	24	9	4	10	21	31	77
46	12	4	7	41	33	2	4	17	19	50	50

1989/90	Barclays Second Division	13th/24
1988/89	Barclays Second Division	15th/24
1987/88	Barclays Second Division	13th/23
1986/87	Today First Division	20th/22
1985/86	Canon First Division	19th/22
1984/85	Canon First Division	15th/22
1983/84	Canon First Division	15th/22
1982/83	English Second Division	3rd/22
1981/82	English Second Division	8th/22
1980/81	English First Division	21st/22
1979/80	English Second Division	1st/22
1978/79	English Second Division	17th/22
1977/78	English First Division	22nd/22
1976/77	English First Division	11th/22
1975/76	English First Division	7th/22
1974/75	English First Division	18th/22
1973/74	English First Division	9th/22
1972/73	English First Division	16th/22
1971/72	English First Division	12th/22
1970/71	English Second Division	1st/22
1969/70	English Second Division	3rd/22
1968/69	English First Division	21st/22
1967/68	English First Division	13th/22
1966/67	English First Division	8th/22
1965/66	English First Division	7th/22
1964/65	English First Division	18th/22
1963/64	English First Division	11th/22
1962/63	English First Division	4th/22
1961/62	English First Division	14th/22

46	10	8	5	34	29	5	6	12	33	50	59
46	11	6	6	31	20	2	10	11	25	43	55
44	12	5	5	35	20	4	6	12	27	41	59
42	9	7	5	39	24	2	2	17	15	52	42
42	7	8	6	35	35	3	4	14	19	41	42
42	10	4	7	39	25	5	2	14	26	48	51
42	11	5	5	40	30	2	7	12	25	38	51
42	11	4	6	36	15	9	6	6	36	29	70
42	12	5	4	31	19	6	7	8	25	29	66
42	7	5	9	20	23	6	1	14	20	44	32
42	12	5	4	32	19	9	8	4	26	19	55
42	7	8	6	28	23	3	9	9	15	29	37
42	4	7	10	16	32	1	5	15	10	38	22
42	8	9	4	30	28	4	9	8	17	32	42
42	9	9	3	29	24	4	10	7	19	27	45
42	8	7	6	25	17	4	5	12	21	43	36
42	10	7	4	35	17	3	9	9	16	24	42
42	7	9	5	23	18	3	8	10	17	28	37
42	9	6	6	18	11	4	7	10	23	35	39
42	12	7	2	30	14	11	6	4	27	16	59
42	12	6	3	37	22	7	7	7	27	28	51
42	8	8	5	27	24	1	4	16	12	44	30
42	7	7	7	37	34	6	5	10	27	35	38
42	12	4	5	47	28	6	4	11	31	43	44
42	12	4	5	40	28	9	3	9	40	37	49
42	9	6	6	43	36	2	7	12	26	49	35
42	9	4	8	33	27	7	7	7	28	31	43
42	14	6	1	53	23	6	6	9	26	30	52
42	12	2	7	38	27	5	4	12	34	44	40

1960/61	English First Division	6th/22
1959/60	English First Division	12th/22
1958/59	English First Division	19th/22
1957/58	English First Division	18th/22
1956/57	English Second Division	1st/22
1955/56	English Second Division	5th/22
1954/55	English First Division	21st/22
1953/54	English Second Division	1st/22
1952/53	English Second Division	5th/22
1951/52	English Second Division	5th/22
1950/51	English Second Division	14th/22
1949/50	English Second Division	15th/22
1948/49	English Second Division	19th/22
1947/48	English Second Division	9th/22
1946/47	English Second Division	9th/22
1938/39	English First Division	22nd/22
1937/38	English First Division	16th/22
1936/37	English Second Division	1st/22
1935/36	English Second Division	6th/22
1934/35	English First Division	21st/22
1933/34	English First Division	17th/22
1932/33	English First Division	19th/22
1931/32	English First Division	19th/22
1930/31	English First Division	16th/22
1929/30	English First Division	8th/22
1928/29	English First Division	2nd/22
1927/28	English First Division	3rd/22
1926/27	English First Division	7th/22
1925/26	English First Division	17th/22

42	12	4	5	54	31	6	5	10	33	39	45
42	8	6	7	38	32	5	7	9	28	43	39
42	7	6	8	34	36	4	4	13	33	62	32
42	11	4	6	59	41	3	1	17	32	71	33
42	14	5	2	68	36	11	6	4	41	31	61
42	15	3	3	63	23	6	3	12	31	55	48
42	9	6	6	43	32	3	5	13	31	54	35
42	15	4	2	63	23	8	6	7	34	37	56
42	13	6	2	55	29	5	6	10	34	45	48
42	12	6	3	48	24	7	3	11	30	40	47
42	10	4	7	42	28	5	7	9	26	30	41
42	8	9	4	30	25	4	6	11	25	40	39
42	6	10	5	41	38	4	6	11	21	41	36
42	10	5	6	36	29	6	6	9	24	28	43
42	11	4	6	42	25	7	3	11	27	39	43
42	7	6	8	35	35	2	5	14	13	47	29
42	9	6	6	31	26	5	5	11	23	49	39
42	14	4	3	56	26	10	4	7	33	31	56
42	14	5	2	53	19	5	5	11	26	38	48
42	9	4	8	39	30	3	5	13	22	56	33
42	10	6	5	36	26	4	5	12	23	48	39
42	9	9	3	43	25	2	4	15	32	64	35
42	11	3	7	46	39	4	4	13	28	55	37
42	12	4	5	50	38	4	2	15	30	57	38
42	12	5	4	57	42	5	4	12	29	48	43
42	16	5	0	67	22	5	4	12	29	45	51
42	14	5	2	66	25	4	7	10	30	47	48
42	13	4	4	58	33	4	8	9	27	37	46
42	11	3	7	42	32	3	7	11	28	48	38

1924/25	English Second Division	1st/22
1923/24	English Second Division	12th/22
1922/23	English Second Division	3rd/22
1921/22	English Second Division	9th/22
1920/21	English Second Division	12th/22
1919/20	English Second Division	14th/22
1914/15	English Second Division One	19th/20
1913/14	English Second Division One	18th/20
1912/13	English Second Division One	15th/20
1911/12	English Second Division One	10th/20
1910/11	English Second Division One	15th/20
1909/10	English Second Division One	5th/20
1908/09	English First Division One	20th/20
1907/08	English Second Division One	2nd/20
1906/07	English Second Division One	3rd/20
1905/06	English Second Division One	7th/20
1904/05	English Second Division One	14th/18
1903/04	English Second Division One	18th/18
1902/03	English Second Division One	15th/18
1901/02	English Second Division One	14th/18
1900/01	English Second Division One	11th/18
1899/00	English Second Division One	5th/18
1898/99	English Second Division One	3rd/18
1897/98	English Second Division One	7th/16
1896/97	English Second Division One	9th/16
1895/96	English Second Division One	8th/16
1894/95	English Second Division One	4th/16

42	15	4	2	58	9	9	7	5	32	23	59
42	13	4	4	43	16	4	4	13	21	38	42
42	14	2	5	42	19	7	7	7	23	25	51
42	11	6	4	30	16	3	11	7	9	18	45
42	10	8	3	26	11	2	8	11	13	35	40
42	8	6	7	26	29	7	4	10	15	32	40
38	6	4	9	31	41	4	0	15	16	47	24
38	7	2	10	29	28	4	2	13	16	33	26
38	12	2	5	34	20	1	5	13	15	45	33
38	11	4	4	34	18	4	3	12	15	48	37
38	12	3	4	37	19	2	2	15	15	43	33
38	15	2	2	60	20	5	2	12	19	38	44
38	6	6	7	32	41	2	3	14	22	61	25
38	14	2	3	41	20	7	8	4	31	27	52
38	15	3	1	44	12	5	5	9	18	27	48
38	10	3	6	30	21	5	9	5	23	27	42
34	8	3	6	30	25	3	4	10	10	30	29
34	5	8	4	26	21	1	2	14	16	61	22
34	5	5	7	20	23	5	3	9	21	42	28
34	11	2	4	26	14	1	3	13	12	42	29
34	9	5	3	30	15	2	5	10	9	22	32
34	11	5	1	34	8	6	4	7	19	28	43
34	12	5	0	35	12	6	4	7	29	30	45
30	8	5	2	26	11	5	2	8	20	24	33
30	11	2	2	44	20	2	2	11	15	37	30
30	10	0	5	40	16	4	4	7	17	28	32
30	11	2	2	45	20	4	6	5	27	33	38

TOP CITY GOALSCORERS

Here are the Foxes' sharp-shooters from over the years – the top 20 all-time top goalscorers (does not include wartime appearances):

Pos	Player	Years	League	FAC	LC	Other	Total	Apps	Ratio
1	Arthur Chandler	1923–1935	259	14	0	0	273	419	0.65
2	Arthur Rowley	1950–1958	251	14	0	0	265	321	0.83
3	Ernie Hine	1926–1932	148	8	0	0	156	259	0.60
4	Derek Hines	1948–1961	116	1	0	0	117	317	0.37
5	Arthur Lochhead	1925–1934	106	8	0	0	114	320	0.36
6	Gary Lineker	1978–1985	95	6	2	0	103	209	0.49
7	Mike Stringfellow	1962–1975	82	7	8	0	97	344	0.28
8	Johnny Duncan	1922–1930	88	7	0	0	95	295	0.32
9	Jimmy Walsh	1956–1964	79	5	5	2	91	199	0.46
10=	Jack Lee	1941–1950	74	10	0	0	84	137	0.61
10=	Alan Smith	1982–1987	76	4	4	0	84	217	0.39
12	Frank Worthington	1972–1977	72	4	2	0	78	239	0.33
13=	Mal Griffiths	1939–1956	66	10	0	0	76	409	0.19
13=	Ken Keyworth	1958–1964	62	7	4	3	76	215	0.35
15	Danny Liddle	1932–1946	64	7	0	0	71	274	0.26
16	Arthur Maw	1932–1939	58	6	0	0	64	189	0.34
17=	Matty Fryatt	2006–2011	51	5	4	2	62	189	0.33
17=	Steve Walsh	1986–2000	53	1	4	4	62	450	0.14
19	Steve Lynex	1981–1987	57	1	2	0	60	240	0.25
20	Fred Shinton	1907–1911	55	3	0	0	58	101	0.57

OTHER NOTABLE CLUB SCORING RECORDS

Most goals
273 by Arthur Chandler

Most League goals
259 by Arthur Chandler

Most goals in first tier (Premier League and predecessors)
203 by Arthur Chandler

Most goals in second tier (Championship and predecessors)
208 by Arthur Rowley

Most goals in third tier (League One and predecessors)
27 by Matty Fryatt

Most FA Cup goals
14 by Arthur Chandler and Arthur Rowley

Most League Cup goals
8 by Mike Stringfellow

TOP GOALSCORERS IN INDIVIDUAL MATCHES AND SEASONS

Most goals scored in a single season
44 by Arthur Rowley (1956/57)

Most goals scored in a season in the first tier (Premier League and predecessors)
34 by Arthur Chandler (1927/28 and 1928/29)

Most goals scored in a season in the second tier (Championship and predecessors)
44 by Arthur Rowley (1956/57)

Most goals scored in a season in the third tier (League One and predecessors)
27 by Matty Fryatt (2008/09)

Most goals scored in one game
6 by Johnny Duncan (*v.* Port Vale, 25 December 1924) and Arthur Chandler (*v.* Portsmouth, 20 October 1928)

Most goals scored on debut
4 by Archie Gardiner (*v.* Portsmouth, 21 February 1934)

OTHER GOALSCORING RECORDS

Most consecutive games scored
8 by Arthur Chandler (6 December 1924–10 January 1925)

Most consecutive League games scored
7 by Arthur Chandler (6 December 1924–3 January 1925) and Arthur Rowley (20 October 1951, December 1951 and 15 December 1956–26 January 1957)

Most hat-tricks (or better)
17 by Arthur Chandler (12x3, 1x4, 3x5, 1x6)

Most penalties scored
41 by Arthur Rowley

Youngest goalscorer
Sixteen years 192 days by Dave Buchanan (*v.* Oldham Athletic, 1 January 1979)

Oldest goalscorer
Forty years 233 days by Kevin Phillips (*v.* Blackpool, 15 March 2014)

Quickest goal
Nine seconds by Matty Fryatt (*v.* Preston North End, 15 April 2006)

Quickest hat-trick
Five minutes by Fred Shinton (*v.* Oldham Athletic, 29 November 1909)

SEQUENCES AND RECORDS

Home League Scoring Records

Highest scoring win
20 October 1928   Leicester City   10-0   Portsmouth

Highest scoring loss
2 January 1932   Leicester City   3-8   Aston Villa

Highest winning margin
20 October 1928   Leicester City   10-0   Portsmouth

Highest losing margin
28 December 1914 Leicester City   0-6   Derby County
15 February 1923   Leicester City   0-6   West Ham United

Highest aggregate

| 21 April 1930 | Leicester City | 6-6 | Arsenal |
| 22 February 1958 | Leicester City | 8-4 | Manchester City |

Highest scoring draw

| 21 April 1930 | Leicester City | 6-6 | Arsenal |

Away League Scoring Records

Highest scoring win

| 14 January 1899 | Luton Town | 1-6 | Leicester City |
| 3 September 1952 | Fulham | 4-6 | Leicester City |

Highest scoring loss

| 21 April 1909 | Nottingham Forest | 12-0 | Leicester City |

Highest winning margin

2 March 1895	Burton United	0-5	Leicester City
14 January 1899	Luton Town	1-6	Leicester City
28 March 1970	Charlton Athletic	0-5	Leicester City

Highest losing margin

| 21 April 1909 | Nottingham Forest | 12-0 | Leicester City |

Highest aggregate

| 21 April 1909 | Nottingham Forest | 12-0 | Leicester City |

Highest scoring draw

29 October 1961	Arsenal	4-4	Leicester City
14 January 1967	Southampton	4-4	Leicester City
22 February 1995	Aston Villa	4-4	Leicester City
22 February 2004	Tottenham Hotspur	4-4	Leicester City

Cup Scoring Records

Highest scoring win
| 1 December 1964 | Coventry City | 1-8 | Leicester City |

Highest scoring loss
| 8 January 1921 | Leicester City | 3-7 | Burnley |
| 27 October 1992 | Sheffield Wednesday | 7-1 | Leicester City |

Highest winning margin
| 9 January 1932 | Leicester City | 7-0 | Crook Town |
| 1 December 1964 | Coventry City | 1-8 | Leicester City |

Highest losing margin
| 27 October 1992 | Sheffield Wednesday | 7-1 | Leicester City |
| 9 October 2001 | Leicester City | 0-6 | Leeds United |

Highest aggregate
10 January 1914	Leicester City	5-5	Tottenham Hotspur
8 January 1921	Leicester City	3-7	Burnley
12 February 1949	Luton Town	5-5	Leicester City

Highest scoring draw
| 10 January 1914 | Leicester City | 5-5 | Tottenham Hotspur |
| 12 February 1949 | Luton Town | 5-5 | Leicester City |

Full League Sequences

Description	Record	Dates
Wins	9	21 Dec 2013–1 Feb 2014
Draws	6	21 Apr 1973–1 Sept 1973
		21 Oct 1976–18 Sept 1976
		2 Oct 2004–2 Nov 2004
Losses	8	17 Mar 2001–28 Apr 2001

Clean sheets	7	14 Febr 1920–27 Mar 1920
Failing to score	7	21 Nov 1987–1 Jan 1988
Without a win	18	12 Apr 1975–1 Nov 1975
Without a draw	44	30 Jan 1909–26 Mar 1910
Without a loss	23	1 Nov 2008–7 Mar 2009
Without a clean sheet	37	9 Feb 1957–26 Dec 1957
Without failing to score	31	12 Nov 1932–28 Oct 1933
		23 Nov 2013–3 May 2014

Home League Sequences

Description	Record	Dates
Wins	13	3 Sept 1906–29 Dec 1906
Draws	5	14 Apr 1903–24 Oct 1903
		25 Oct 1967–23 Dec 1967
		19 Apr 1975–13 Sept 1975
Losses	5	3 Jan 1959–18 Mar 1959
Clean sheets	6	14 Mar 1925–2 May 1925
		16 Dec 1950–10 Mar 1951
		11 Mar 1972–22 Apr 1972
Failing to score	5	21 Oct1971–2 Oct 1971
		30 Apr 1983–10 Sept 1983
Without a win	12	22 Nov 2003–24 Apr 2004
Without a draw	37	1 Dec 1894–27 Mar 1897
Without a loss	40	12 Feb 1898–17 Apr 1900
Without a clean sheet	25	18 Sept 1948–12 Nov 1949
Without failing to score	50	18 Apr 1927–26 Oct 1929

Away League Sequences

Description	Record	Dates
Wins	5	21 Dec 2013–1 Feb 2014
Draws	5	1 Oct 1921–19 Nov 1921
		26 Feb 2005–9 Apr 2005
Losses	15	18 Oct 1986–2 May 1987
Clean sheets	5	27 Feb 1971–3 Apr 1971

Failing to score	5	23 Mar 1901–12 Oct 1901
		8 Apr 1905–23 Sept 1905
		26 Dec 1913–28 Feb 1914
		18 Oct 1919–13 Dec 1919
		13 Oct 1968–21 Sept 1968
		14 Jan 1978–14 Mar 1978
		28 Nov 1987–16 Jan 1988
		26 Sept 2001–17 Nov 2001
Without a win	23	19 Nov 1988–4 Nov1989
Without a draw	21	24 Nov 1951–25 Oct 1952
Without a loss	13	21 Dec 2013–26 Apr 2014
Without a clean sheet	33	5 Apr 1901–10 Apr 1903
Without failing to score	22	15 Oct 1932–14 Oct 1933

CITY AND CUP FINALS: THE RECORD SO FAR

Season	Competition	Details
1968/1969	FA Cup	Man City 1-0 Leicester
1962/1963	FA Cup	Man United 3-1 Leicester
1960/1961	FA Cup	Spurs 2-0 Leicester
1948/1949	FA Cup	Wolves 3-1 Leicester
1999/2000	League Cup	Leicester 2-1 Tranmere Rovers
1998/1999	League Cup	Spurs 1-0 Leicester
1996/1997	League Cup	Leicester 1-0 'Boro
1964/1965	League Cup	First leg: Leicester 0-0 Chelsea
		Second leg: Chelsea 3-0 Leicester
		(Chelsea win 3-2)
1963/1964	League Cup	First leg: Stoke 1-1 Leicester
		Second leg: Leicester 3-2 Stoke
		(Leicester wins 4-3)
1971/1972	FA Charity Shield	Leicester City 1-0 Liverpool
		(at Filbert Street)

CITY'S ALL-TIME LEAGUE RECORD

In this fascinating table, the complete record of all 141 clubs who have taken part in English League football, City lie in twenty-third position overall, and at the start of the 2014/15 campaign, were twenty games away from 4,500 matches. City

			Home		
		P	W	D	L
1	Manchester United	4404	1350	479	373
2	Liverpool	4372	1347	488	351
3	Arsenal	4372	1294	514	378
4	Preston North End	4730	1254	599	512
5	Wolverhampton Wndrs	4670	1267	540	528
6	Sheffield United	4584	1220	582	490
7	Burnley	4706	1250	578	525
8	Everton	4496	1239	548	461
9	Manchester City	4446	1251	489	483
10	Aston Villa	4508	1248	520	486
11	Sunderland	4538	1234	559	476
12	Blackburn Rovers	4580	1225	543	522
13	Notts County	4756	1172	603	603
14	West Bromwich Albion	4628	1173	562	579
15	Bolton Wanderers	4614	1234	537	536
16	Derby County	4624	1230	532	550
17	Newcastle United	4404	1247	481	474
18	Nottingham Forest	4540	1140	578	552
19	Sheffield Wednesday	4544	1205	550	517
20	Bristol City	4384	1158	568	466
21	Bury	4622	1153	598	560
22	Birmingham City	4534	1150	575	542
23	Leicester City	4480	1119	584	537
24	Chelsea	3994	1063	511	423
25	Blackpool	4472	1091	585	560

have scored 6,731 goals up to the start of the new season and, remarkably, conceded 6,735 – a difference of just four goals! The Foxes are above the likes of Spurs, West Ham and Leeds United in the all-time table, though Nottingham Forest are currently five places higher – for now!

Away

F	A	W	D	L	F	A	GD	Pt
4489	2075	765	568	869	3158	3512	+2060	6028
4596	2126	725	576	885	2883	3247	+2106	5883
4424	2123	703	577	906	2905	3399	+1807	5757
4366	2657	579	602	1184	2670	4001	+378	5442
4570	2652	618	565	1152	2905	4211	+612	5437
4252	2535	610	557	1125	2755	4046	+426	5389
4303	2606	568	571	1214	2630	4293	+34	5336
4402	2480	607	578	1063	2706	3780	+848	5334
4448	2523	581	581	1061	2790	3840	+875	5282
4466	2536	612	564	1078	2840	3973	+797	5271
4266	2428	587	540	1142	2758	4038	+558	5227
4348	2633	552	593	1145	2647	4159	+203	5218
4148	2681	570	583	1225	2623	4254	-164	5197
4305	2717	610	577	1127	2800	4086	+302	5192
4197	2529	545	580	1182	2644	4110	+202	5189
4491	2766	556	581	1175	2591	4096	+220	5185
4330	2470	558	553	1091	2597	3789	+668	5178
3908	2506	565	594	1111	2653	3896	+159	5144
4155	2550	534	593	1145	2620	4016	+209	5130
3841	2224	532	572	1088	2422	3764	+275	5106
4011	2609	555	546	1210	2588	4069	-79	5099
3977	2499	549	566	1152	2531	3911	+98	5052
4100	2674	549	580	1111	2613	4061	-22	5023
3668	2203	596	525	876	2522	3245	+742	4984
3866	2550	541	556	1139	2547	3961	-98	4938

ALL-TIME FA CUP TABLE

City's FA Cup record leaves a bit more to be desired, lying thirty-fifth out of 250. Here is the complete record (with three points for a win for table purposes) with the teams that lie above:

		P	W	D	L
1	Manchester United	420	227	96	97
2	Arsenal	429	227	102	100
3	Everton	416	224	82	110
4	Liverpool	412	217	91	104
5	Chelsea	378	196	91	91
6	Tottenham Hotspur	398	201	99	98
7	Aston Villa	409	212	80	117
8	Manchester City	337	165	69	103
9	Blackburn Rovers	394	191	86	117
10	Peterborough United	215	103	48	64
11	West Bromwich Albion	382	184	82	116
12	Newcastle United	359	170	85	104
13	Bolton Wanderers	385	179	90	116
14	Sheffield Wednesday	392	181	94	117
15	Swindon Town	290	140	50	100
16	Preston North End	346	164	65	117
17	Wolverhampton Wndrs	370	170	84	116
18	Sheffield United	360	161	89	110
19	Darwen	63	30	8	25
20	Derby County	332	151	62	119
21	Watford	280	124	62	94
22	Bournemouth	251	110	59	82
23	Huddersfield Town	261	117	52	92
24	Walsall	261	114	60	87
25	West Ham United	314	132	85	97
26	Burnley	338	145	78	115
27	Southampton	330	140	80	110

Key: CS = clean sheet kept, NG = failed to score, PPG = points per game average

CS	NG	F	A	GD	PTS	PPG
150	83	760	472	+288	777	1.85
154	88	729	445	+284	783	1.83
146	74	757	465	+292	754	1.81
170	103	682	393	+289	742	1.80
136	73	680	401	+279	679	1.80
126	75	767	479	+288	702	1.76
113	80	832	527	+305	716	1.75
110	74	607	424	+183	564	1.67
128	85	733	466	+267	659	1.67
62	45	375	292	+83	357	1.66
116	81	672	454	+218	634	1.66
114	81	623	445	+178	595	1.66
126	81	650	502	+148	627	1.63
108	78	692	497	+195	637	1.63
91	64	509	400	+109	470	1.62
102	89	663	450	+213	557	1.61
100	78	658	472	+186	594	1.61
113	91	533	439	+94	572	1.59
16	15	157	117	+40	98	1.56
90	68	605	513	+92	515	1.55
93	59	440	378	+62	434	1.55
73	66	429	338	+91	389	1.55
74	72	399	327	+72	403	1.54
83	68	392	336	+56	402	1.54
86	75	476	415	+61	481	1.53
96	87	568	461	+107	513	1.52
95	79	513	426	+87	500	1.52

28	Nottingham Forest	380	159	97	124
29	Wimbledon	132	54	36	42
30	Sunderland	343	144	82	117
31	Ipswich Town	201	85	44	72
32	Notts County	333	144	63	126
33	Aldershot	169	71	38	60
34	Port Vale	264	110	61	93
35	Leicester City	286	120	62	104

ALL-TIME LEAGUE CUP RECORD: TOP TWENTY

City have fared best in the competition they have enjoyed most over the years, the League Cup. In fact, only six clubs have won the trophy more than City. The Foxes, with three League Cup trophies under their belt, are twelfth of 118 clubs who have taken

1	Liverpool	216	125	49	42
2	Aston Villa	231	135	44	52
3	Tottenham Hotspur	200	118	34	48
4	Arsenal	214	120	46	48
5	Manchester United	183	105	29	49
6	Manchester City	197	104	38	55
7	Nottingham Forest	189	96	44	49
8	West Ham United	207	108	39	60
9	Norwich City	200	102	42	56
10	Chelsea	184	92	41	51
11	Everton	166	79	40	47
12	Leicester City	171	85	30	56
13	Queens Park Rangers	165	82	27	56
14	Sheffield Wednesday	165	79	36	50
15	Southampton	186	87	45	54
16	Ipswich Town	167	81	31	55

121	94	615	492	+123	574	1.51
44	41	163	162	+1	198	1.50
101	76	550	456	+94	514	1.50
60	49	319	275	+44	299	1.49
91	78	605	486	+119	495	1.49
49	41	277	257	+20	251	1.49
62	64	403	377	+26	391	1.48
85	68	433	406	+27	422	1.48

part in the competition over the past fifty-five years – not bad at all. They have Chelsea and Everton in the sights as a place in the top ten beckons. Using the key above and the same scoring system, here is the list as it stood at the start of the 2014/15 campaign:

80	33	436	211	+225	424	1.96
79	37	457	270	+187	449	1.94
78	29	391	211	+180	388	1.94
81	38	396	213	+183	406	1.90
64	34	324	203	+121	344	1.88
67	45	374	228	+146	350	1.78
65	40	363	220	+143	332	1.76
65	41	384	257	+127	363	1.75
66	44	342	235	+107	348	1.74
56	32	333	222	+111	317	1.72
59	32	300	180	+120	277	1.67
56	38	287	231	+56	285	1.67
49	37	302	217	+85	273	1.65
43	35	277	210	+67	273	1.65
66	46	322	223	+99	306	1.65
39	33	282	227	+55	274	1.64

17	Coventry City	159	79	22	58
18	Blackburn Rovers	172	80	37	55
19	Leeds United	172	84	25	63
20	Birmingham City	192	89	42	61

ZENITH DATA SYSTEMS/FULL MEMBERS

		P	W	D	L
1	Nottingham Forest	15	11	1	3
2	Ipswich Town	22	15	2	5
3	Chelsea	27	18	3	6
4	Middlesbrough	17	11	0	6
5	Everton	15	9	2	4
6	Crystal Palace	23	14	1	8
7	Southampton	13	8	0	5
8	Blackburn Rovers	13	8	0	5
9	Leicester City	12	6	2	4
10	Bradford City	11	6	0	5

PLAY-OFF ALL-TIME TABLES:

1	Hull City	3	3	0	0
2	Burnley	3	3	0	0
3	Swansea City	3	2	1	0
4	Notts County	3	2	1	0
5	Queens Park Rangers	3	2	1	0
6	Swindon Town	8	6	0	2
7	Blackpool	6	4	1	1
8	West Ham United	9	6	1	2
9	Bristol City	3	2	0	1
10	Leicester City	16	8	4	4

46	35	273	236	+37	259	1.63
42	32	304	237	+67	277	1.61
52	41	289	229	+60	277	1.61
47	42	318	260	+58	309	1.61

CUP ALL-TIME TABLE

CS	FtS	F	A	GD	Pt	PPG
3	0	35	19	+16	34	2.27
6	3	42	29	+13	47	2.14
8	4	55	41	+14	57	2.11
4	3	29	19	+10	33	1.94
3	0	36	25	+11	29	1.93
4	5	44	33	+11	43	1.87
4	1	24	14	+10	24	1.85
4	3	21	16	+5	24	1.85
3	4	17	14	+3	20	1.67
3	1	20	17	+3	18	1.64

CHAMPIONSHIP TOP TEN

2	0	7	1	+6	9	3.00
3	0	4	0	+4	9	3.00
1	1	7	3	+4	7	2.33
1	0	5	2	+3	7	2.33
2	1	3	1	+2	7	2.33
2	1	15	11	+4	18	2.25
1	0	13	10	+3	13	2.17
5	2	14	5	+9	19	2.11
0	1	4	3	+1	6	2.00
6	4	24	17	+7	28	1.75

THE FINAL WORD...

Quotes from the boss

Nigel Pearson guided City back to the Promised Land when he helped the club to promotion in 2013/14 – here are some of the more unusual quotes from the Foxes chief.

On managing City:

I have always seen my long-term future, and that of my staff, at Leicester City. On the back of the success we have worked so hard to achieve, I have always been confident that my future would remain here. I feel very proud to be the manager of a club with genuine ambition, a clear direction in which it wants to go and loyal owners that are prepared to support its development.

On hiking:

That's my escapism. I like being out there. I've done Snowdon, walked a bit of the Cleveland Way, did some of the Coast to Coast. When I was younger, I did the Yorkshire Three Peaks - Pen-y-ghent, Whernside, Ingleborough – and then half the Pennine Way but the lad I was doing it with got called into the Air Force, so we binned it. He went to the Falklands, helicopter mechanic. I would have gone into the Forces if it hadn't been for football. RAF.

On keeping out of the media circus:

I have a normal life, I have a sense of humour. I don't live in the Leicester area on purpose. I live in Sheffield. I got the train in this morning. I had a walk yesterday afternoon and went to the pub in the evening. My family is very important to me. If you ask the staff here I'm a nightmare to get hold of with the phone at times. I might choose to have a day when I'm not available but I'll have my emails. I have an understanding of how much is at stake in football, how much money is at stake, how much investment there is and what it means to the fans. It's an emotional game. It's a focal point for communities. It's escapism for fans. Sport is a wonderful thing but it is just that: sport. It is my job.

On pressure:

I love football but I remember working with Sam Allardyce at Newcastle and he said, 'I ****ing hate match-days.' I know where he's coming from. The nerves. The emotion. Getting the preparation right. That build-up to the game is horrible. This job is love-hate. It motivates me but also brings the worst out of me. It's like being a masochist.

On avoiding hot water:

I'm a good actor. People ask me: 'Why aren't you on the bench? Why are you up there in the stands?' I made a few flippant remarks because I know it irritates people. It started when I got sent off against Charlton. I just walked over to the ref and told him what I thought (about Matty James being sent off and a foul on Kasper Schmeichel). I said, 'You're a ****ing disgrace.' I got a two-game ban, sat in the stand and thought 'I'll stay up there'. Bloody-minded. 'I can't get sent off from here,' I said to the media, a flippant, silly remark. I am up there now because there's expectancy that if you're English to show passion. I can be like that but actually I want to view the game. I probably have a better chance of affecting the game by seeing what I see and passing the message on.

Some Sports Stand the Test of Time

Classic Guides

from Amberley Publishing

Find us on Facebook
facebook.com/amberleybooks

Follow us on Twitter
@amberleybooks

W. www.amberley-books.com   T. +44 1453 847800   E. sales@amberley-books.com